Phonics They Use

Words for Reading and Writing

FOURTH EDITION

Patricia M. Cunningham

Wake Forest University

PEARSON

Boston   New York   San Francisco
Mexico City   Montreal   Toronto   London   Madrid   Munich   Paris
Hong Kong   Singapore   Tokyo   Cape Town   Sydney

Series Editor: Aurora Martínez Ramos
Series Editorial Assistant: Erin Beatty
Senior Marketing Manager: Elizabeth Fogarty
Production Administrator: Michael Granger
Editorial-Production Service: Omegatype Typography, Inc.
Manufacturing Buyer: Andrew Turso
Composition Buyer: Linda Cox
Cover Administrator: Linda Knowles
Interior Design: Denise Hoffman
Electronic Composition: Omegatype Typography, Inc.

For related titles and support materials, visit our online catalog at www.ablongman.com.

Library of Congress Cataloging-in-Publication Data

Cunningham, Patricia Marr.
    Phonics they use : words for reading and writing / Patricia M. Cunningham.—4th ed.
      p. cm.
    Includes bibliographical references and index.
    ISBN 0-205-41037-5
    1. Reading—Phonetic method. 2. English language—Study and teaching (Elementary)—Activity programs. I. Title.
LB1573.3.C86 2005
    372.46'5—dc22

                                      2003070679

Brief Contents

Contents

v

part two

Fluency   53

 ## Fluency Activities   54

 ## High-Frequency Words   64

part three

Using Phonics and Spelling Patterns   85

 ## Making Words   87

part four

Big Words 125

part five

Coaching, Assessment, Research, and Jargon 161

Introduction

When this book first appeared in 1991, very few reading gurus—my best friends included—gave it much of a chance. Phonics was not something you talked about, and most people believed (or pretended to believe) that teachers had stopped doing it! Somehow the first edition sold enough copies to allow it to be revised and the second edition appeared just as people were beginning once again to talk about phonics. As this fourth edition appears, my concerns about phonics have done a complete about-face! Underemphasized in 1991, it now dominates the curriculum in many schools. I think of the old Beatles' song, "All You Need Is Love!" When people talk about teaching children to read, they are often saying, "All you need is phonics!" Phonics is an important part of any balanced reading program—but it is only one part. It is necessary but not sufficient! Children need to be reading and writing, to be read to, and to be taught how to comprehend what they read. A balanced reading program has some of all the necessary components to turn children into avid, thoughtful readers and writers. In this fourth edition of *Phonics They Use,* I have redoubled my efforts to remind you that what matters is not how much phonics they know—but what they actually use when they need it for decoding a new word while reading and spelling a new word while writing.

The biggest change in this edition is its new organization. Instead of four very long chapters that reviewers told me were "daunting" to many students and teachers, there are now 15 shorter and hopefully "less daunting" chapters. Each chapter has been thoroughly updated and contains some of the best activities from prior editions along with some new ideas and activities.

Part One has four chapters that together will help you establish a firm foundation for all children to learn to read. Chapter One defines five critical understandings children must develop to start their journey down the literacy road: what reading and writing are for; print concepts; phonological and phonemic awareness; concrete words; and letter names and sounds. Three activities—shared reading of predictable books, predictable charts, and writing—are described to build these early reading concepts.

Chapter Two details how writing, predictable charts, and shared reading activities can be extended to develop print concepts. Getting to Know You is an activity that focuses on the children in your class and uses your children's names and information about the children to further develop print concepts.

Phonological and phonemic awareness is the focus of Chapter Three. Children develop their phonological awareness as they learn to count words and clap syllables. Their phonemic awareness is developed as they participate in the activities designed to develop the concept of rhyme and teach blending and segmenting. Activities are also included using the children's names to build phonological and phonemic awareness.

Chapter Four contains activities to build children's store of concrete words and to teach letter names and sounds. Activities in this chapter include focusing on the names, using alphabet books, learning foods and actions to solidify letter sounds, establishing key words for sounds and two very popular activities we call Changing a Hen to a Fox and Guess the Covered Word. Chapter Four ends with an explanation of how all the activities contained in the first four chapters are multilevel.

Part Two has two chapters that provide activities for helping children learn to read and write fluently. Chapter Five suggests classroom-tested ways to develop fluency. Children become fluent readers as they engage in lots of independent reading, write daily, and participate in some repeated reading activities. A Fluency Development Lesson, which can be easily included in any teaching setting, is described.

Chapter Six describes activities for teaching high-frequency words. In English, a little over 100 words account for every other word we read and write. Most of these words are abstract, meaningless, connecting words. Many of them have irregular spellings and pronunciations. Chapter Six describes ways to build meaning for these words and explains how to use a word wall so that children learn to automatically and rapidly identify these words while reading and spell them while writing. Chapter Six ends with an explanation of how all the fluency and word-wall activities are multilevel.

Part Three contains activities that will help children use patterns to decode words. In Chapter Seven, you will learn how Making Words can help all levels of children move forward in their decoding and spelling abilities. Chapter Eight focuses on rhyming patterns with a variety of activities you can use to teach children to decode and spell using patterns. Chapter Nine presents two activities—Word Sorting and Hunting and What Looks Right?—to help children become sensitive to spelling patterns. The final section in Chapter Nine describes how all the decoding and spelling activities are multilevel.

Part Four emphasizes the need for children to learn to read and spell some big words so that they have in their heads examples for the patterns found in big words. The chapters in Part Four will help children build a store of big words and help them learn to use their big words to decode, spell, and build meaning for unfamiliar big words.

Because children love to collect things, Chapter Ten is on helping children become word collectors. Activities are suggested for both class and personal collections. In addition to becoming word collectors, children are encouraged to become word detectives, seeking out clues in words by comparing them to other words they know. Chapter Eleven focuses on roots, prefixes, and suffixes—the building blocks of many polysyllabic words in English.

Part Five includes chapters on coaching, assessment, research, and jargon. In Chapter Twelve, I share some strategies teachers use for coaching children to use what they know when they need it—when they are actually reading and writing. Chapter Thirteen includes assessment devices that focus not just on what children know about phonics but also on what they actually use while reading and writing. Everything in *Phonics They Use* is grounded in the research literature, and the pertinent research is summarized in Chapter Fourteen. The final chapter summarizes some of the major jargon teachers are expected to know. This chapter cautions you to not use too much of this jargon with your children because it tends to confuse them and takes their attention away from what you are really trying to teach them. Teachers, however, are expected to know this jargon and the final chapter provides you with a handy reference.

I am indebted to all the wonderful teachers who have shared their ideas and adaptations of ideas for making phonics instruction both informative and entertaining. I hope this new edition of *Phonics They Use* will continue to support them in providing the best, most multilevel, and transfer-oriented phonics instruction possible. I am also indebted to all the reviewers who offered suggestions on both small and grand ways to make the book better: Gwynne Ash, University of Delaware; Melise Bunker, Palm Beach Atlantic College; Jeanne Cobb, Eastern New Mexico University; Linda Conrad, Baldwin Wallace College; Mary Jane Eisenhauer, Purdue North Central; and Charles MacArthur, University of Delaware.

part
one

Building the
Foundation
for Phonics
They Can
Use

Part One has four chapters that together will help you establish a firm foundation for all children to learn to read. Chapter One defines five critical understandings children must develop to start their journey down the literacy road:

What reading and writing are for
Print concepts
Phonological and phonemic awareness
Concrete words
Letter names and sounds

Three activities—shared reading of predictable books, predictable charts, and writing—are described to build these early reading concepts.

Chapter Two details how writing, predictable charts, and shared reading activities can be extended to develop print concepts. Getting to Know You is an activity that focuses on the children in your class and uses your children's names and information about the children to further develop print concepts.

Phonological and phonemic awareness is the focus of Chapter Three. Children develop their phonological awareness as they learn to count words and clap syllables. Their phonemic awareness is developed as they participate in the activities designed to develop the concept of rhyme and teach blending and segmenting. Activities are also including using the children's names to build phonological and phonemic awareness.

Chapter Four contains activities to build children's store of concrete words and to teach letter names and sounds. Activities in this chapter include focusing on the names, using alphabet books, learning foods and actions to solidify letter sounds, establishing key words for sounds, and two very popular activities we call Changing a Hen to a Fox and Guess the Covered Word. Chapter Four ends with an explanation of how all the activities contained in the first four chapters are multilevel.

Early Reading and Writing Activities

Before we begin helping children learn letter–sound relationships they can use, we must be sure our children know what they are trying to learn and how it is useful to them. There is a tremendous amount of research, usually included under the term *emergent literacy* (Teale & Sulzby, 1991), which shows us what happens in the homes of children where literacy is a priority. We know that children born into homes where someone spends time with them in reading and writing activities walk into our schools with an incredible foundation on which our instruction can easily build. These children experience an average of over 1,000 hours of quality one-on-one reading and writing activities.

Parents (or parent substitutes including grandmothers, aunts, uncles, brothers, and sisters) read to children and talk with them about what they are reading. This reading is usually done in the lap position, where the child can see the pictures as well as the words used to tell about the pictures. Favorite books are read again and again and eventually most children opt for a book that they pretend-read—usually to a younger friend or a stuffed animal.

In addition to reading, these children are exposed to writing at an early age. They scribble and make up ways to spell words. They ask (and are told) how to spell favorite words. They make words with magnetic letters and copy favorite words from books. From the over 1,000 hours of reading and writing experiences, these children learn some incredibly important concepts. These concepts include:

What reading and writing are for
Print concepts
Phonological and phonemic awareness
Concrete words
Letter names and sounds

Early Reading Concepts

What Reading and Writing Are For

Imagine you are visiting in a first-grade classroom. You have a chance to talk with several children and ask them, "Why are you learning to read and write?" Some children answer, "You have to learn to read and write." When pushed, they can name all kinds of "real-world" things as reasons for reading and writing—books, newspapers, magazines, recipes, and maps. Other children respond to the why-learn-to-read-and-write question with answers such as, "to do your workbook," "to read in reading group," and "to go to second grade." Children who give "school-world" answers to this critical question demonstrate that they don't see reading and writing as part of their real world. Children who don't know what reading is for in the real world do not have the same drive and motivation as children for whom reading and writing, like eating and sleeping, are things everyone does. In addition, children who pretend-read a memorized book and "write" a letter to Grandma are confident they can read and write!

Print Concepts

Print is what you read and write. Print includes all the funny little marks—letters, punctuation, space between words and paragraphs—that translate into familiar spoken language. In English, we read across the page in a left-to-right fashion. Because our eyes can see only a few words during each stop (called a fixation), we must actually move our eyes several times to read one line of print. When we finish that line, we make a return sweep and start all over again, left to right. If there are sentences at the top of a page and a picture in the middle and more sentences at the bottom, we read the top first and then the bottom. We start at the front of a book and go toward the back. These arbitrary rules about how we proceed through print are called *conventions*.

Jargon refers to all the words we use to talk about reading and writing. Jargon includes such terms as *word, letter, sentence,* and *sound.* We use this jargon constantly as we try to teach beginners to read:

> "Look at the *first word* in the *second sentence.* How does that *word begin*? What *letter* has that *sound*?"

Using some jargon is essential to talking with children about reading and writing, but children who don't come from rich literacy backgrounds are often very confused by this jargon. Although all children speak in words, they don't know words exist as separate entities until they are put in the presence of reading and writing. To many children, letters are what you get in the mailbox, sounds are horns and bells and doors slamming, and sentences are what you have to serve if you get caught committing a crime! These children are unable to follow our "simple" instructions because we are using words for which they have no meaning or an entirely different meaning.

Many children come to school knowing these print concepts. From being read to in the lap position, they have noticed how the eyes "jump" across the lines of print as someone is reading. They have watched people write grocery lists and thank-you notes to Grandma and have observed the top–bottom, left–right movement. Often, they have typed on the computer and observed these print conventions. Because they have had someone to talk with them about reading and writing, they have learned much of the jargon.

While writing down a dictated thank-you note to Grandma, Dad may say, "Say your sentence one word at a time if you want me to write it. I can't write as fast as you can talk." When the child asks how to spell *birthday,* he may be told, "It starts with the letter *b,* just like your dog Buddy's name. *Birthday* and *Buddy* start with the same sound and the same letter."

Children with reading and writing experiences know how to look at print and what teachers are talking about as they give them information about print. All children need to develop these critical understandings in order to learn to read and write.

Phonological and Phonemic Awareness

Phonological awareness and *phonemic awareness* are terms that refer to children's understandings about words and sounds in words. *Phonological awareness* is the broader term and includes the ability to separate sentences into words and words into syllables. Phonemic awareness includes the ability to recognize that words are made up of a discrete set of sounds and to manipulate sounds. Phonemic awareness is important because children's level of phonemic awareness is highly correlated with their success in beginning reading (Ehri & Nunes, 2002; National Reading Panel, 2000). Phonological awareness develops through a series of stages during which children first become aware that language is made up of individual words, that words are made up of syllables, and that syllables are made up of phonemes. It is important to note here that it is not the "jargon" children learn. Five-year-olds cannot tell you there are three syllables in *dinosaur* and one syllable in *Rex*. What they can do is clap out the beats in *dinosaur* and the one beat in *Rex*. Likewise, they cannot tell you that the first phoneme in *mice* is "mmm," but they can tell you what you would have if you took the *mmm* off *mice—ice*. Children develop this phonemic awareness as a result of the oral and written language they are exposed to. Nursery rhymes, chants, and Dr. Seuss books usually play a large role in this development.

Phonemic awareness is an oral ability. You hear the words that rhyme. You hear that *baby* and *book* begin the same. You hear the three sounds in *bat* and can say these sounds separately. Only when children realize that words can be changed and how changing a sound changes the word are they able to profit from instruction in letter–sound relationships.

Children also develop a sense of sounds and words as they try to write. In the beginning, many children let a single letter stand for an entire word. Later, they put more letters and often say the word they want to write, dragging out its sounds to hear what letters they might use. Children who are allowed and encouraged to "invent-spell" develop an early and strong sense of phonemic awareness.

Concrete Words

If you sit down with first graders on the first day of school and try to determine if they can read by giving them a new book to read or testing them on some common words such as *the, and, of,* or *with,* you would probably conclude that most first graders can't read yet. But many first graders can read and write some words. Here are some words a boy named David could read when he began first grade:

> David
> Mama
> Daddy
> Bear Bear (his favorite stuffed animal)
> Carolina (his favorite basketball team)
> Pizza Hut
> I love you (written on notes on good days)
> I hate you (written on notes on bad days)

Most children who have had reading and writing experiences have learned 10 to 15 words. The words they learn are usually concrete words that are important to them. Being able to read these words is important, not because they can read much with these few words, but because children who come to school already able to read or write some concrete words have accomplished an important and difficult task. They have learned how to learn words.

Letter Names and Sounds

Finally, many children have learned some letter names and sounds. They may not be able to recognize all 26 letters in both upper- and lowercase and they often don't know the sounds of *w* or *v*, but they have learned the names and sounds for the most common letters. Usually, the letter names and sounds children know are based on those concrete words they can read and write.

The Foundation

From the research on emergent literacy, we finally understand what we mean when we say a child is "not ready." We know that many preschoolers have hundreds of hours of literacy interactions during which they develop understandings critical to their success in beginning reading. We must now structure our school programs to try to provide for all children what some children have had. This will not be an easy task. We don't have 1,000 hours, and we don't have the luxury of doing it with one child at a time, and when the child is interested in doing it! But we must do all we can, and we must do it in ways that are as close to the home experiences as possible. In the remainder of the chapters in Part One, I describe activities successfully used by kindergarten and first-grade teachers who are committed to putting all children in the presence of reading and writing and allowing all children to learn:

> What reading and writing are for
> Print concepts
> Phonological and phonemic awareness
> Concrete words
> Letter names and sounds

For older children just acquiring English, these understandings are also critical for them to develop the foundation on which reading and writing can grow.

 # Shared Reading of Predictable Books

Teachers of young children have always recognized the importance of reading a variety of books to children. There is one particular kind of book and one particular kind of reading, however, that have special benefits for building the reading and writing foundations—shared reading with predictable Big Books.

Shared reading is a term used to describe the process in which the teacher and the children read a book together. The book is read and reread many times. On the first several readings, the teacher usually does all of the reading. As the children become more familiar with the book, they join in and "share" the reading.

Predictable books are the best kind of books to use with shared reading. Predictable books are books in which repeated patterns, refrains, pictures, and rhyme allow children to "pretend-read" a book that has been read to them several times. Pretend reading is a stage most children go through with a favorite book that some patient adult has read and reread to them. Perhaps you remember pretend reading with such popular predictable books as *Goodnight Moon, Are You My Mother?,* or *Brown Bear, Brown Bear.* Shared reading of predictable books allows all children to experience this pretend reading. From this pretend reading, they learn what reading is, and they develop the confidence that they will be able to do it. They also develop print concepts and begin to understand how letters, sounds, and words work.

In choosing a book for shared reading, consider three criteria. First, the book must be very predictable. The most important goal for shared reading is that even children with little experience with books and stories will be able to pretend-read the book after several readings and develop the confidence that goes along with that accomplishment. Thus, you want a book without too much print and one in which the sentence patterns are very repetitive and the pictures support those sentence patterns.

Second, you want a book that will be very appealing to the children. Since the whole class of children will work with the same Big Book, and since the book will be read and reread, you should try to choose a book that many children will fall in love with.

Finally, the book should take you someplace conceptually. Many teachers choose Big Books to fit their units, build units around the books, or share Big Books by the same author or illustrator to study style.

Shared reading is called "shared" because we want children to join in the reading. There are many ways to encourage children to join in. Many teachers read the book to the children the first time and then just invite the children to join in when they can on subsequent reading. You might also want to "echo read" the book, with you reading each line and then the children being your echo and reading it again. Some teachers like to read the book with the children several times and then make a tape recording in which the teacher reads some parts and the whole class or groups of children read the other parts. Children delight in going to the listening center and listening to themselves reading the book!

In addition to books, many teachers write favorite poems, chants, songs, and finger plays on long sheets of paper and these become some of the first things children can actually read. Most teachers teach the poem, chant, song, or finger play to the children first. Once the children have learned to say, chant, or sing it, they then are shown what the words look like. The progression to reading is a natural one and children soon develop the critical "of course, I can read" self-confidence. Once children can read the piece, many teachers copy it and send it home for the child to read to parents and other family members.

Once the book has been read, enjoyed, and reread in a variety of ways, most children will be able to read (or pretend-read) most of the book. This early "I can read" confidence is critical to emerging readers and the shared book experience as described is a wonderful way to foster this. When engaging in shared reading with predictable Big Books, we try to simulate what would happen in the home as a child delights in having a favorite book read again and again. First, we focus on the book itself, on enjoying it, rereading it, talking about it, and often acting it out. As we do this, we develop concepts and oral language. When most of the children can pretend-read the book, we focus their attention on the print. We do writing activities related to the book and help children learn print conventions, jargon, and concrete words. When children know some concrete words, we use these words to begin to build phonemic awareness and letter–sound knowledge. The remaining chapters in Part One will provide more detail on building on the shared reading experience to develop these important concepts.

Predictable Charts

Just as children enjoy reading predictable books together, they also like to write and read predictable charts. A predictable chart is created by the teacher and children. What makes it predictable is that all the sentences begin with the same stem. Each child's response completes the sentence. Figure 1.1 shows a predictable chart made by a class after their visit to the fair.

Writing a predictable chart is a natural follow-up to a predictable book, a field trip, or a new topic or theme. *Things I Like* by Anthony Browne is about a little chimp who tells about all the things he likes—painting, riding a bike, playing with toys. After reading and enjoying *Things I Like* by Anthony Browne, the teacher and children talked about things they liked and recorded these on a Things I Like chart. The teacher usually begins the chart by telling something he or she likes.

I like reading books. (Miss Williams)

Next, each child tells something he or she likes to do. The teacher writes their sentences on the chart and places each child's name after the sentence in parentheses. After sharing their likes on the Things I Like chart, children are delighted to share what they don't like to do, resulting in a Things I Don't Like chart, as shown in Figures 1.2 and 1.3.

At the Fair

I saw rides. (Mr. Bland)
I saw animals. (Paul)
I saw baby cows. (Hannah)
I saw apples. (Mary)
I saw horses. (John)
I saw goats. (Lowell)
I saw sheep. (Laura)
I saw food. (Melissa)
I saw ponies. (Ryan)
I saw candy apples. (Suzanne)
I saw games. (Michelle)

I saw a big pumpkin. (Jamarcio)
I saw chickens. (Angelica)
I saw cows. (José)
I saw an elephant. (Chad C.)
I saw a big slide. (Chad B.)
I saw a merry-go-round. (Kristen)
I saw cakes and pies. (Karen)
I saw lots of people. (Matthew)
I saw some pigs. (Zannie)
I saw some corn. (Jasmine)

FIGURE 1.1
At the Fair Predictable Chart

Source: Hall, D., & Williams, E. (2001). *Predictable charts: Shared writing for kindergarten and first grade.* Greensboro, NC: Carson-Dellosa. Used with permission from Carson-Dellosa Publishing Company's CD-2410, Predictable Charts.

School

In school I like to read. (Mr. Parker)
In school I like to write. (Jackie)
In school I like to do the calendar. (Vincent)
In school I like to learn. (Janice)
In school I like centers. (Benjamin)

FIGURE 1.2
Things I Like Predictable Chart

Source: Hall, D., & Williams, E. (2001). *Predictable charts: Shared writing for kindergarten and first grade.* Greensboro, NC: Carson-Dellosa. Used with permission from Carson-Dellosa Publishing Company's CD-2410, Predictable Charts.

Things I Do Not Like To Do

I do not like to clean up. (Mr. Robson)
I do not like to sing. (Laura)
I do not like to wait in line. (Diane)
I do not like to play football. (Angie)
I do not like to play t-ball. (Joe)

FIGURE 1.3
Things I Don't Like Predictable Chart

Source: Hall, D., & Williams, E. (2001). *Predictable charts: Shared writing for kindergarten and first grade.* Greensboro, NC: Carson-Dellosa. Used with permission from Carson-Dellosa Publishing Company's CD-2410, Predictable Charts.

Friends
My friend is Pat. (Mrs. Moore)
My friend is Sharon. (Arthur)
My friend is Jim. (David)
My friend is Chris. (John)
My friend is Joey. (Kevin)

Thanksgiving
I am thankful for a good class. (Mrs. Kump)
I am thankful for good food. (Bob)
I am thankful for friends. (Bobby)
I am thankful for horses. (Kathy)
I am thankful for books. (Laura)

In a People House
You see chairs. (Mrs. Greene)
You see beds. (Glenda)
You see pictures. (Rusty)
You see dishes. (Katherine)
You see towels. (Gray)

Sports
My favorite sport is basketball. (Mrs. Hall)
My favorite sport is soccer. (Sarah)
My favorite sport is swimming. (Alex)
My favorite sport is baseball. (Joannie)
My favorite sport is gymnastics. (Dennis)

At the Library
My favorite book is Bats. (Mrs. Gingras)
My favorite book is Stellaluna. (Karen)
My favorite book is Curious George. (Genny)
My favorite book is Rainbow Fish. (Sue)
My favorite book is Madeline. (Robby)

FIGURE 1.4
More Ideas for Predictable Charts

Source: Hall, D., & Williams, E. (2001). *Predictable charts: Shared writing for kindergarten and first grade.* Greensboro, NC: Carson-Dellosa. Used with permission from Carson-Dellosa Publishing Company's CD-2410, Predictable Charts.

There is no limit to the different topics that can be turned into predictable charts. Figure 1.4 includes just a few examples to show you how versatile this early reading format is.

When the predictable chart is completed, the teacher reads it to the children or has each child read his or her own sentence to the class. Children can do this because they know how each sentence starts and that it finishes with what they said.

Writing

Until recently, kindergarten and first-grade children were often not allowed or encouraged to write until they could make most of the letters correctly and spell lots of words. The theory was that if children were allowed to write before they could spell and make the letters correctly, they would acquire "bad habits" that later would be hard to break. There is a certain logic in this argument, but this logic does not hold up to scrutiny when you actually look at children before they come to school.

Just as children from literacy-oriented homes read before they can read by pretend-reading a memorized book, they write before they can write! Their writing is usually not readable by anyone besides them, and sometimes they read the same scribbling different ways. They write with pens, markers, crayons, paint, chalk, and with normal-sized pencils with erasers on the ends! They write on chalkboards, magic slates, walls, drawing paper, and lined notebook paper. (They just ignore the lines!)

They write in scribbles, which first go anywhere and then show a definite left-to-right orientation. They make letterlike forms. They underline certain letters to show word boundaries. As they learn more about words and letters, they let single letters stand for entire words. They draw pictures and intersperse letters with the pictures.

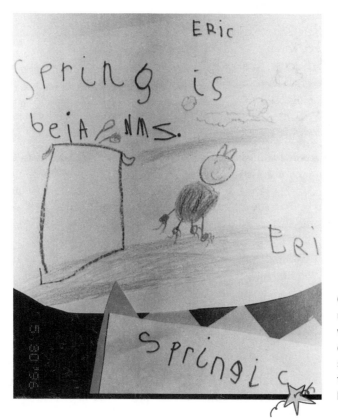

Children develop crucial understandings as they write, copying some words displayed in the room and stretching out other words to put down sounds they hear.

They make grocery lists by copying words off packages. They copy favorite words from books. They write love notes (e.g., "I love you, Mama").

Emergent literacy research has shown us that children are not ruined by being allowed to write before they can write. Rather, they learn many important concepts and develop the confidence that they can write (Sulzby, Teale, & Kamberelis, 1989). Here are some activities that promote writing for all.

Provide a Print-Rich Classroom

Classrooms in which children write contain lots of print in them. In addition to books, there are magazines and newspapers. Charts of recipes made and directions for building things hang as reminders. Children's names are on their desks and on many different objects. There are class books, bulletin boards with labeled pictures of animals under study, and labels on almost everything. Children's drawings and all kinds of writing are displayed. In these classrooms, children see that all kinds of writing is valued. Equally important, children who want to write "the grown-up way" can find lots of words to make their own.

Let Children Watch You Write

As children watch you write, they observe that you always start in a certain place, go in certain directions, and leave space between words. In addition to these print conventions, they observe that writing is "talk written down." There are numerous opportunities in every classroom for the teacher to write as the children watch—and sometimes help—with suggestions of what to write.

In many classrooms, the teacher begins the day by writing a morning message on the board. The teacher writes this short message as the children watch. Some ideas for morning messages are shown in Figure 1.5.

The teacher then reads the message, pointing to each word and inviting the children to join in on any words they know. Sometimes teachers take a few minutes to point out some things students might notice from the morning message:

"How many sentences did I write today?"

"How can we tell how many there are?"

"What do we call this mark I put at the end of this sentence?"

"Do we have any words that begin with the same letters?"

"Which is the longest word?"

These and similar questions help children learn print tracking and jargon and focus their attention on words and letters.

Messages about the weather

Dear Class,
It is raining today.
I love you.
Miss Williams

Messages about school events, especially in the first weeks

Dear Class,
The principal will visit today.
I love you.
Miss Williams

Messages about places you visit or social studies

Dear Class,
We will go to the fire station today.
I love you.
Miss Williams

Seasonal messages (Johnny Appleseed in late September)

Dear Class,
Today is Tuesday.
We will make apple sauce today.
I love you.
Miss Williams

Messages connected to reading

Dear Class,
Today is Wednesday.
We will read "Humpty Dumpty" today.
I love you.
Miss Williams

Messages connected to math

Dear Class,
Today is Monday.
We will graph our favorite colors.
I love you.
Miss Williams

FIGURE 1.5
Morning Messages

Source: Hall, D., & Williams, E. (2003). *Writing mini-lessons for kindergarten.* Greensboro, NC: Carson-Dellosa. Used with permission from Carson-Dellosa Publishing Company.

Include Interactive Writing

Interactive writing is described by Pinnell and Fountas (1998) as "sharing the pen." This notion of not only letting children tell you what to write but also letting them "share the pen" is what makes interactive writing different from watching the teacher write and what makes it important to include as another writing format.

To do interactive writing, you gather the children up close to you at a chart or the board and with the children you think of something you want to write. For beginning lessons, what you write should be quite short—nor more than a sentence or two. Perhaps you and the children decide that you should write about Brad's birthday and that the sentences should say,

Today is Brad's birthday. He is six years old.

You then might ask children to look around the room and see if they can find the word *today* anywhere. When a child finds the word *today*, that child is given the pen and comes up and writes *Today*—the first word in the sentence.

The writing continues as the teacher asks if anyone can come up and write *is*. Brad comes and writes his name. The teacher adds the apostrophe and Brad adds the *s*. Together the teacher and children stretch out *birthday*. Different children come and write the letters they can hear and the teacher fills in the other letters to get *birthday* spelled correctly. Another child volunteers to come and put the period to show that we have finished the first sentence. The same procedure is continued with the second sentence. Children who can spell *he* and *is* come and write those words. *Six* is found on the number chart and someone comes and writes *six*. *Years* and *old* are stretched out with volunteers writing letters they can hear and the teacher filling in missing letters. Finally, a child adds the period at the end of the second sentence. Children love "sharing the pen" and they pay much more attention to the writing when they are a part of it. Regular, short interactive writing sessions should be a part of every young child's day.

Let Them Write and Accept Whatever Kind of Writing They Do

Accepting a variety of writing—from scribbling to one-letter representations, to invented spellings, to copied words—is the key to having young children write before they can write. Sometimes it is the children and not the teacher who reject beginning attempts. If more advanced children give the less advanced children a hard time about their "scribbling," the teacher must intervene and firmly state a policy, such as:

"There are many different ways to communicate through writing. We use pictures and letters and words. Sometimes we just scribble, but the scribbling helps us remember what we are thinking. We use all these different ways in this classroom!"

Without this attitude of acceptance, the very children who most need to explore language through writing will be afraid to write.

Encouraging young children to write has many benefits. As children write, they learn the print concepts of left to right and leaving spaces between words. (Even when children are scribbling, they usually scribble from left to right and stop occasionally to write a new scribble.) Children often write about themselves and each other and copy names of favorite foods, restaurants, and places from the print in the classroom. From these writing opportunities, they learn concrete, important-to-them words. As they stretch out words to "put down the sounds they hear," they are developing phonemic awareness. We are all more apt to remember things we actually use. As children use what they are learning about letters and sounds to try to spell words, they are applying their phonics knowledge. Writing is perhaps our best opportunity for developing young children's print concepts, concrete words, phonemic awareness, and knowledge of letters and sounds. Because they are writing what they want to tell, they also become perfectly clear about what reading and writing are for.

 ## Summary

In order to make sense of phonics instruction, children must develop some basic concepts. They must know why people read and write and develop an "I can't wait 'til I can do it too" attitude. They must learn how to track print and understand the print-related jargon used to talk about print. They also need to develop a basic level of phonological and phonemic awareness, learn some important-to-them words, and learn some letter names and sounds. This chapter has suggested three activities—shared reading of predictable Big Books, predictable charts, and writing—which will help children begin to develop these basic concepts. The remaining chapters in Part One will focus specifically on print concepts, phonological and phonemic awareness, and learning some words, letter names, and sounds.

Developing Print Concepts

As described in Chapter One, print concepts include print tracking and print jargon. Children need to become automatic at tracking print and understanding the words we use to talk about reading and writing so that they can focus their attention on learning to read and write. All three activities described in Chapter One can help children develop print concepts.

Using Writing to Develop Print Concepts

Writing is the most "visible" way to develop print concepts. As children watch you write the morning message or sentences on a chart, they see print tracking in operation. You can make these concepts more obvious by pointing out and "thinking aloud" about what you are doing as you are doing it. Here are some of the common "think-alouds" done by teachers that help children pay attention to print concepts as they watch the teacher write. (Jargon and concepts are bolded and should be emphasized as you say them.)

"Today I am going to write two **sentences** to tell you about what will happen at 10:00.

"I start the first **word** of my **sentence** with a capital **letter.**"

Teacher writes *We,* saying "We" as she writes it.

"I need a **space** before my next **word.**"

Teacher puts a "finger space" and then writes *will.* Each word is read by the teacher as she writes it.

"Another finger **space** and I can write the third **word** of my **sentence.**"

Teacher writes *have.*

"This **word** is also a **letter** and takes only one **letter** to spell it."

Teacher writes *a.*

"The next word is a **long word** and takes **seven letters** to spell it."

Teacher writes *special.*

"The **last word** in my **sentence** is . . ."

Teacher writes and says "*treat.*"

"I am at the **end** of my **first sentence** so I will put a **period** here to show that. I have one more **sentence** to write. I will write it on this **second line** and **start back on the left** again."

Teacher writes:

Bobby's mom is bringing cupcakes for his birthday!

As she writes, she talks about what she is doing as she did for the first sentence.

As the year goes on, instead of telling the children what she is doing, she asks them what she should do, with questions such as:

"I am writing the **first word** in my **sentence.** What kind of **letter** do I need?"

"I have finished my **first word.** What do I need to leave **between the first word and the next word**?"

"I am at the **end of my sentence.** What should I put here to show that?"

"I am going to write another **sentence. Where should I start** writing it?"

Because children can actually watch you write and see the message go down one letter and word at a time, many people believe that modeling writing for children is one of the most effective ways to teach print concepts.

Letting the children write—in whatever way they can—is another powerful way to teach print concepts. As the children write, the teacher circulates and encourages children—coaching them with gentle prompts:

"I will put a little dot here on the **left side** to help you start your sentence in the right place."

"You have the word *I* written. Tell me the rest of your sentence."

Child tells sentence, "I like my cat." Teacher says,

"Good. Put a finger space here and then write your second word *like*. Can you find *like* in the room to spell it or should we stretch it out?"

"Is that the end of your sentence? What do you need to put at the end of your sentence?"

"Are you going to write another sentence? Where will you begin it?"

Some teachers hesitate to let children write before they know much about reading and writing because the writing is far from perfect. It helps many teachers to remember that when young children are writing, it doesn't matter what it looks like when they finish. What matters are all the understandings they are developing as they go through the process. Writing provides the "teachable moment" to teach print concepts and all young children should be encouraged and applauded for their early writing efforts.

Using Predictable Charts to Develop Print Concepts

Predictable charts are a reading and writing activity with powerful potential to develop print concepts. After writing the chart with the children and rereading it several times, many teachers copy the sentences of the chart on sentence strips. Each sentence is then cut into words and the words are distributed to various children. The children then come to the front and get themselves in the right order to make the sentence. The child whose sentence is being constructed is always given his or her name and goes to the end of the sentence. We call this activity Sentence Builders, and children delight in becoming the words to make their sentences along with the sentences of their friends. See Figure 2.1 for an example based on a "Fruits I Like" predictable chart.

FIGURE 2.1
Children Building a Sentence from the Fruits Predictable Chart
Source: Hall, D., & Williams, E. (2001). *Predictable charts: Shared writing for kindergarten and first grade.*
Greensboro, NC: Carson-Dellosa. Used with permission from Carson-Dellosa Publishing Company.

Another activity many teachers use is called What Do You Notice? On the day after the chart was written, the children read the chart again, with each child reading his or her own sentence. Next, the teacher asks children to look at the sentences and come up and point to things they notice. Children will notice a variety of things depending on what they know about letters, sounds, words, and reading. These may include:

"All sentences begin with **I Like.**"
"**Pears** and **peaches** begin with the same letter."
"**Ryan's** and **Refugio's** names start with a capital **R.**"
"**I** is at the beginning of every sentence!"
"**I** is always a capital (or big) letter."
"**Watermelon** is the biggest word."
"All sentences have this (pointing to all the periods) at the end."

Whatever the children notice is accepted and praised by the teacher. The teacher also asks more questions:

"Who can find a fruit that is on our chart more than once?"
"Who can find any other words that begin like **peaches** and **pears**?"

Friends

My friend is Pat. (Mrs. Moore)

My friend is Sharon. (Arthur)

My friend is Jim. (David)

My friend is Chris. (John)

My friend is Joey. (Kevin)

FIGURE 2.2

Friends Predictable Chart and Cover and Page from Class Book

Source: Hall, D., & Williams, E. (2001). *Predictable charts: Shared writing for kindergarten and first grade.* Greensboro, NC: Carson-Dellosa. Used with permission from Carson-Dellosa Publishing Company's CD-2410, Predictable Charts.

In addition to doing Sentence Builders and What Do You Notice?, many teachers help the children construct class books based on the predictable charts, like that shown in Figure 2.2. The words cut apart during the Sentence Builders are recycled for this activity. Children are given the words to their sentence (in an envelope or clipped together). They place their words in correct order along the bottom of a large sheet of drawing paper. Once someone has checked that the words are in the correct order (with none upside down!), the child pastes the words down. Each child illustrates his or her sentence and the pages are bound together into a class book.

 # Using Shared Reading to Develop Print Concepts

Chapter One described shared reading as a major opportunity for teachers to help children develop confidence in and desire to learn to read and write. Once a Big Book has been read, talked about, reread, and enjoyed several times, you can use that book to develop print concepts. What Do You Notice? and Sentence Builders are again the activities most commonly used.

What Do You Notice? is done exactly as described in the previous section on predictable charts. Teachers choose pages from the Big Book. The children and teacher reread the pages. Children volunteer to come up and point out what they notice. If no one notices something the teacher thinks is important, she asks the "Who can come and find?" question to prompt them to pay attention to that feature.

For Sentence Builders, we often pick a few pages from the book and write the sentences for those pages on sentence strips. Once the sentences are cut apart into words, they are given to children who come up and become the words to build the sentences.

For a predictable book such as *Brown Bear, Brown Bear, What Do You See?*, the children can have all the words in the book and make all the pages. This is one activity that it is better for the teacher not to prepare ahead of time. Children need to be involved in deciding which words to write on the cards and which words they already have, and they also need to watch the teacher writing them. Here is how the words for *Brown Bear* might get written.

The teacher and children reread the first page of *Brown Bear* and the teacher asks the children to tell her what words and punctuation marks to write on the cards. Directed by the children, she prints one to a card these words:

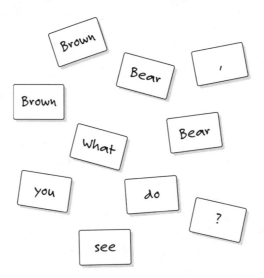

The teacher places these words in order along the chalk ledge or in a pocket chart and the children read the sentence chorally.

The teacher turns the page and tells the children that she wants to write all the words and punctuation marks needed to make the sentence on this page but not write again any words already written. The children decide that she needs a card for:

I

But not for *see* which is already written; one for

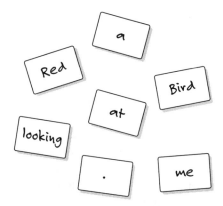

This sentence is then constructed taking the *see* out of the first sentence.

The process speeds up as the children realize that just a few words need to be written for each of the remaining pages. The words not already written from previous sentences are written as needed and each sentence is built along the chalk ledge or in the pocket chart. Each sentence is also read chorally as one child points to the words to be read.

Once the book is completed, you have all the words and punctuation marks needed to do Sentence Builders for each sentence in *Brown Bear*. Distribute all the cards to all the children, giving several words to some children if necessary. Go back to the beginning of the book and have the class read the sentence chorally as the children who have cards with words or punctuation marks in that sentence come up and build that sentence. Children love being the words and making the sentences. Equally important, they learn important print concepts in a very concrete way.

Getting to Know You

Most teachers begin their year with some get-acquainted activities. As part of these get-acquainted activities, they often have a special child each day. In addition to learning about each child, you can focus attention on the special child's name and use the name to develop some important understandings about words and letters.

To prepare for this activity, write all the children's first names (with initials for last names if two names are the same) with a permanent marker on sentence strips. Cut the strips so that long names have long strips and short names have short strips. Let the children watch you write their names and have them help you spell their names if they can. After writing each name, display it in a pocket chart or other board.

As you put each name up, comment on letters shared by certain children or other common features:

> "Rasheed's name starts with an *r* just like Robert's."
>
> "Bo's name only takes two letters to write. He has the shortest name but he is one of the tallest boys."
>
> "We have two Ashleys so I will have to put the first letter of her last name—M—so that we will know which Ashley this is."

We want the children to watch and think as the names are being written and they usually will because they are so egocentric—interested in themselves and in each other. Their attention for anything, however, diminishes after 15–20 minutes so if you have a large class, you may want to write the names in two different sessions.

Once you have all the names written and displayed, ask volunteers to come and find a name they can read. Many children will read their own and almost everyone will remember *Bo*!

Tell the children that each day one of them will be the special child and that in order to make it fair—because some children will have to wait 20 or more days—you are going to put all the names in a box and shake up the box and, without looking, draw one of the names. Tell the children what the special child will get to do each day. Some teachers crown that child king or queen, let them lead the line, decide what game to play for P.E., sit in a special chair to greet visitors, pass things out, take messages to the office, and so on. Do keep in mind that whatever you do for the first, you must do for all the rest, so make sure you can sustain whatever you start. (Remember the "Don't do anything the first month of marriage you don't want to do the whole rest of your married life" advice most of us got but ignored!) Each day, reach into the box and draw out a name. This child becomes the special child and the focus of many literacy activities. For our example, we will assume that David is the first name pulled from the box.

Interviewing and Shared Writing

Have David come up and sit in a special chair and appoint the rest of the class reporters. Their job is to interview David and find out what he likes to eat, play, and do after school. Does he have brothers? Sisters? Cats? Dogs? Mice? Decide on a certain number of questions (5–7) and call on different children to ask the questions.

After the interview, write your "newspaper article" on this special child using a shared writing format in which the children give suggestions and you and they decide what to say first, last, and so on. Record this on a chart while the children watch. The chart should not be more than 5–6 sentences long and the sentences should not be too complex because these articles about each VIP will form some of the first material most children will be able to read. The interview and the writing of the chart should be completed in the 20-minute attention span and can be if the teacher limits the number of questions and takes the lead in the writing of the article. This first activity for each child—interviewing and shared writing of the article—develops crucial oral language skills and helps children see how writing and reading occur.

Shared Reading of the Charts

The second activity is the reading of David's chart. This takes place later in the day and, again, does not take more than 20 minutes. On the first day, you will only have one chart to read. Lead the children to read it chorally several times and let volunteers come and read each sentence. Guide their hands so that they are tracking print as they read. Most teachers display each chart for five days and then let the child take the chart home with instructions to display it on the child's bedroom door. That way, there are only five charts in the room at any one time but every chart gets read and reread on five different days.

Many teachers also write (or type) the article from the chart and, after all the children have had their special days and have been interviewed, compile a class book containing each article (often along with a picture of each child). Each child then has one night to take the book home so that the family can get to know the whole class.

Developing Print Concepts

As the children watch you write each child's chart, they once again have an opportunity to see writing happening and observe print concepts. To make sure their attention is focused on print tracking and print jargon, you can do Sentence Builders and What Do You Notice? activities based on the children's charts. Young children are very egocentric and they don't need to be reminded to pay attention when the subject of each day's lesson is them and their friends.

 Summary

In order to become fluent readers and writers, children must become automatic at tracking print and understanding the print-related meanings of words such as *letter, word, sentence, beginning, end, first, last, same,* and many others. This chapter has described how shared reading, predictable charts, writing, and Getting to Know You activities can be used to develop these important concepts.

chapter 3

Phonological and Phonemic Awareness

As described in Chapter One, phonological and phonemic awareness refers to children's understandings about words and sounds in words. Phonological awareness includes the ability to separate sentences into words and words into syllables. Phonemic awareness includes the ability to recognize that words are made up of a discrete set of sounds and to manipulate sounds. Many children come to school with well-developed phonemic awareness abilities and these children usually come from homes in which rhyming chants, jingles, and songs are part of their daily experience. These same chants, jingles, and songs should be a part of every young child's day in the classroom. Children also develop a sense of sounds and words as they try to write. Children who are allowed and encouraged to "invent-spell" develop an early and strong sense of phonemic awareness.

Many of the activities discussed in Chapters One and Two help children develop phonemic awareness. As they participate in shared reading and writing, they become aware of words as separate entities. Sentence Builders and What Do You Notice? both help children understand what words are. Encouraging invented spelling during writing is one of the main ways teachers have of helping children develop their understanding of how phonemes make up words. As children try to spell words, they say them slowly, listening to themselves saying the sounds and thinking about what they are learning about letters and sounds. Following are other activities you can use to promote phonological and phonemic awareness.

Developing Phonological Awareness

Phonological awareness includes the ability to separate sentences into words and words into syllables. Two activities, counting words and clapping syllables, help develop children's phonological awareness.

Count Words

To count words, all children should have 10 counters in a paper cup. (Anything manipulable is fine. Some teachers use edibles such as raisins, grapes, or small crackers and let the children eat their counters at the end of the lesson. This makes cleanup quick and easy.) Begin by counting some familiar objects in the room (windows, doors, trash cans), having all children place one of their counters on their desks as each object is pointed to. Have children return counters to the cup before beginning to count the next object.

Tell children that you can also count words by putting down a counter for each word you say. Explain that you will say a sentence in the normal way and then repeat the sentence, pausing after each word. The children should put down counters as you slowly say the words in the sentence and then count the counters and decide how many words you said. As usual, children's attention is better if you make sentences about them. ("Carol has a big smile. Paul is back at school today. I saw Jack at the grocery store.") Once the children catch on to the activity, let them say some sentences, first in the normal way, then one word at a time. Listen carefully as they say their sentences the first time because they will often need help saying them one word at a time. Children enjoy this activity, and not only are they learning to separate out words in speech, but they are also practicing counting skills.

Clap Syllables

Once children can automatically separate the speech stream into words, they are ready to begin thinking about separating words into some components. The first division most children learn to make is that of syllables. Clapping seems the easiest way to get every child involved, and the children's names (what else?) are the naturally appealing words to clap. Say the first name of one child. Say the name again, and this time, clap the syllables. Continue saying first names and then clapping the syllables as you say them the second time, and invite the children to join in clapping with you. As children catch on, say some middle or last names. The term *syllables* is a little jargony and foreign to most young children, so you may want to refer to the syllables as beats. Children should realize by clapping that *Paul* is a one-beat word, *Miguel* is a two-beat word, and *Madeira* is a three-beat word.

Once children can clap syllables and decide how many beats a given word has, help them to see that one-beat words are usually shorter than three-beat words—that is, they take fewer letters to write. To do this, write on sentence strips some words children cannot read and cut the strips into words so that short words have short strips and long words have long strips. Have some of the words begin with the same letters but be different lengths so that children will need to think about word length to decide which word is which.

For the category *animals,* you might write *horse* and *hippopotamus; dog* and *donkey; kid* and *kangaroo;* and *rat, rabbit,* and *rhinoceros.* Tell the children that you are going to say the names of animals and they should clap to show how many beats the word has. (Do not show them the words yet!) Say the first pair, one at a time *(horse, hippopotamus)* and have the children say them. Help children to decide that *horse* is a one-beat word and *hippopotamus* takes a lot more claps and is a five-beat word. Now, show them the two words and say, "One of these words is *horse* and the other is *hippopotamus.* Who thinks they can figure out which one is *horse* and which one is *hippopotamus?*" Help the children by explaining that because *hippopotamus* takes so many beats to say it, it probably takes more letters to write it. Continue with other pairs—and finally with a triplet—*rat, rabbit, rhinoceros*—to make it more multilevel.

Developing the Concept of Rhyme

Recognizing and producing rhyming words is an essential part of phonemic awareness. To develop the concept of rhyme, teachers use nursery and other rhymes and take advantage of all the wonderful rhyming books.

Do Nursery Rhymes

One of the best indicators of how well children will learn to read is their ability to recite nursery rhymes when they walk into the kindergarten. Since this is such a reliable indicator, and since rhymes are so naturally appealing to children at this age, kindergarten classrooms should be filled with rhymes. Children should learn to recite these rhymes, sing the rhymes, clap to the rhymes, act out the rhymes, and pantomime the rhymes. In some kindergarten classrooms, they develop "raps" for the rhymes.

Once the children can recite many rhymes, nursery rhymes can be used to teach the concept of rhyme. The class can be divided into two halves—one half says the rhyme but stops when they get to the last rhyming word. The other half waits to shout the rhyme at the appropriate moment:

First half:	There was an old woman who lived in a shoe. She had so many children, she didn't know what to
Second half:	do.
First half:	She gave them some broth without any bread, and spanked them all soundly and put them to
Second half:	bed.

Nursery and other rhymes have been a part of our oral heritage for generations. Now we know that the rhythm and rhyme inherent in nursery rhymes are important vehicles for the beginning development of phonemic awareness. They should play a large role in any kindergarten curriculum.

Do Rhymes and Riddles

Young children are terribly egocentric, and they are very "body oriented." In doing rhymes and riddles, therefore, have children point to different body parts to show rhyming words. Tell children that you are going to say some words that rhyme with *head* or *feet*. After you say each word, have the children repeat the word with you and decide if the word rhymes with *head* or *feet*. If the word you say rhymes with *head*, they should point to their head. If it rhymes with *feet*, they should point to their feet. As children point, be sure to respond, acknowledging a correct response by saying something like, "Carl is pointing to his head because *bread* rhymes with *head.*" You may want to use some of these words:

meet	bread	led	sleet	seat	red	sheet	fed
bed	beat	sled	thread	dead	greet	heat	shed

Now, ask the children to say the missing word in the following riddles (the answers all rhyme with *head*):

On a sandwich, we put something in between the . . .
When something is not living anymore, it is . . .
To sew, you need a needle and . . .
The color of blood is . . .
We can ride down snowy hills on a . . .

Here are other riddles, the answers to which rhyme with *feet:*

> Steak and pork chops are different kinds of . . .
> On a crowded bus, it is hard to get a . . .
> You make your bed with a . . .
> When you are cold, you turn on the . . .

If children like this activity, do it again, but this time have them listen for words that rhyme with *hand* or *knee.* If the word you say rhymes with *hand,* they should point to their hand. If it rhymes with *knee,* they should point to their knee. Some words to use are:

sand	band	land	see	me	bee	stand
grand	we	free	brand	tea	tree	and

Here are some riddles for *hand:*

> At the beach, you dig in the . . .
> To build a house, you must first buy a piece of . . .
> The musicians who march and play in a parade are called a . . .
> You can sit or you can . . .

And some more that rhyme with *knee:*

> You use your eyes to . . .
> You could get stung by a . . .
> If something doesn't cost anything, we say it is . . .
> You can climb up into a . . .

To challenge your class, have them make up riddles and point for words that rhyme with *feet, knee, hand,* or *head.* As each child gives a riddle, have the riddle giver point to the body part that rhymes with the answer. Model this for the children by doing a few to show them how.

Sing Rhymes and Read Lots of Rhyming Books

There are many wonderful rhyming books, but because of its potential to develop phonemic awareness, one deserves special mention. Along with other great rhyming books, Dr. Seuss wrote *There's a Wocket in My Pocket.* In this book, all kinds of Seussian creatures are found in various places. In addition to the wocket in the pocket, there is a vug under the rug, a nureau in the bureau, and a yottle in the bottle! After several readings, children delight in chiming in to provide the nonsensical word and scary creature that lurks in harmless-looking places. After reading the book a few times, it is fun to decide what creatures might be lurking in your classroom. Let children make up the creatures, and accept whatever they say as long as it rhymes with their object:

> "There's a pock on our clock!"
>
> "There's a zindow looking in our window!"
>
> "There's a zencil on my pencil!"

Once you have found some wonderful books with lots of rhymes, follow these steps to assure your children are learning to recognize and produce rhymes:

1. Pick a book with lots of rhymes that you think your children will "fall in love with." Read, enjoy, and talk about the content of the book, and let children become thoroughly comfortable and familiar with the book. Remember that children who are lucky enough to own books want books read to them again and again.

2. Once the children are very familiar with the book, reread it again, and tell them that the author of this book made it "fun to say" by including lots of rhymes. Read

There are lots of wonderful rhyming books that can be used to develop phonemic awareness. Here are a few of our favorites:

Any rhyming book by Dr. Seuss
There's a Wocket in My Pocket (Dr. Seuss, Random House, 1974)
The Hungry Thing (Jan Slepian and Ann Seidler, Scholastic, 1988)
"I Can't," Said the Ant (Polly Cameron, Coward, 1961)
Jake Baked the Cake (B. G. Hennessey, Viking, 1990)
Pretend You're a Cat (Jean Marzollo, Dial, 1990)
Ape in a Cape (Fritz Eichenberg, Harcourt, 1952)
Catch a Little Fox (Beatrice De Regniers, Scholastic, 1968)
Buzz Said the Bee (Wendy Lewison, Scholastic, 1992)
Moose on the Loose (Carol Ochs, Carolrhoda, 1991)
Down by the Bay (Raffi, Crown, 1987)
There's a Bug in My Mug and *My Nose Is a Hose* (Kent Salisbury, McClanahan, 1997)

the book, stopping after each rhyme, and have children identify the rhyming words and say them with you.

3. For the next reading, tell children that you are going to stop and have them fill in the rhyming word. Read the whole book, stopping each time and having children supply the rhyming word.

4. The activities in steps 2 and 3 have helped children identify rhymes. We also want children to produce rhymes. Depending on the book, find a way to have children make up similar rhymes. Producing rhymes was what children were doing when they made up rhyming items such as "the zencil on the pencil."

Recognizing and producing rhymes is one of the critical components of phonemic awareness. Children who engage in these kinds of activities with wonderful rhyming books will develop the concept of rhyme.

Teaching Blending and Segmenting

Blending is the ability to put sounds back together to form words. Segmenting is the ability to separate a word into its component sounds. Blending and segmenting are difficult concepts for many children but they can develop them if you use lots of blending and segmenting games, tongue twisters, and sound boxes.

Play Blending and Segmenting Games

In addition to hearing and producing rhyme, the ability to put sounds together to make a word—blending—and the ability to separate out the sounds in a word—segmenting—are critical components of phonemic awareness. Blending and segmenting are not easy for many children. In general, it is easier for them to segment off the beginning letters (the onset) from the rest of the word (the rime) than it is to separate all the sounds. In other words, children can usually separate *bat* into *b-at* before they can produce the three sounds *b-a-t*. The same is true for blending. Most children can blend *S-am* to produce the name *Sam* before they can blend *S-a-m*. Most teachers begin by having children blend and segment the onset from the rime and then move to blending and segmenting individual letters.

There are lots of games children enjoy that can help them learn to blend and segment. The most versatile is a simple riddle guessing game. The teacher begins the game by naming the category and giving the clue:

"I'm thinking of an animal that lives in the water and is a *f-ish*." (or *f-i-sh*, depending on what level of blending you are working on)

The child who correctly guesses *fish* gives the next riddle:

"I'm thinking of an animal that goes quack and is a *d-uck*." (or *d-u-ck*)

This sounds simplistic, but children love it, and you can use different categories to go along with units you are studying.

A wonderful variation on this guessing game is to put objects in a bag and let children reach in the bag to choose one. Then they stretch out the name of the object and call on someone to guess "What is it?" Choose small common objects you find in the room—a cap, a ball, chalk, a book. Let the children watch you load the bag and help you stretch out the words for practice as you put them in.

Children also like to talk like "ghosts." One child chooses an object in the room to say as a ghost would, stretching the word out very slowly: "dddoooorrr." The child who correctly guesses *door* gets to ghost talk another object—"bbboooookkk." The ghost-talk game and the guessing game provide practice in segmenting and blending as children segment words by stretching them out and other children blend the words together to guess them.

Tongue Twisters and Books with Lots of Alliteration

In addition to concepts of rhyme, blending, and segmenting, children must learn what it means that words "start the same." This understanding must be in place before children can make sense of the notion that particular letters make particular sounds. Many children confuse the concept of words beginning or starting with the same sound with the concept of rhyme, so many teachers like to wait until the concept of rhyme is firmly

These three practical books give you lots of "fun" activities for helping children develop phonemic awareness:

Phonemic Awareness: Playing with Sounds to Strengthen Beginning Reading Skills
    (J. Fitzpatrick, Creative Teaching Press, 1997)
The Phonological Awareness Handbook for Kindergarten and Primary Teachers
    (L. Ericson and M. F. Juliebo, International Reading Association, 1998)
Phonics through Poetry: Teaching Phonemic Awareness Using Poetry
    (B. B. Hajdusiewicz, Goodyear, 1998)

established for most children before focusing on whether or not words begin with the same sound. Just as for rhyme, we would build a lot of our work with words that start the same by choosing wonderful books such as *All About Arthur—an Absolutely Absurd Ape* by Eric Carle. Arthur, an ape who plays the accordion, travels around the country meeting lots of other musicians—including, in Baltimore, a bear who plays a banjo, and a yak in Yonkers. *Dr. Seuss's ABC,* in which each letter of the alphabet has a sentence such as "Many mumbling mice are making midnight music in the moonlight," is another excellent example of an appealing book that helps children understand what it means to "start the same." In using alliterative books, we would follow the same steps followed with rhyming books:

1. Read and enjoy the book several times.
2. Point out that the author used some "start the same" words to make the book fun to say and identify these words.
3. Let the children say the "start the same" words with you as you read the book again.
4. Have the children come up with other words that "start the same" that the author could have used on that page.

Once you have read and enjoyed several tongue-twister books, why not create a tongue-twister book for your class? Let the children help you make up the tongue twisters and add two or three each day. Turn them into posters or bind them into a class book and let the children read them with you several times—as slowly as they can and as fast as they can. Help the children understand that what makes tongue twisters hard to say fast is that the words all start the same and you keep having to get your mouth and tongue into the same place. The same first sound repeated over and over is also what makes them so much fun to say. Here are some to get you started. You and your children can surely make up better ones. Be sure to use children's names from your class when they have the right letters and sounds!

Billy's baby brother bopped Betty.
Carol can catch caterpillars.
David dozed during dinner.
Fred's father fell fifty feet.
Gorgeous Gloria gets good grades.
Hungry Harry hates hamburgers.
Jack juggled Jill's jewelry.
Kevin's kangaroo kicked Karen.
Louie likes licking lemon lollipops.
Mike's mom makes marvelous meatballs.
Naughty Nellie never napped nicely.
Patty picked pink pencils.

Tongue-Twister Books

Here are some wonderful tongue-twister books:

Faint Frogs Feeling Feverish and Other Terrifically Tantalizing Tongue Twisters
(Lillian Obligada, Viking, 1983)
All About Arthur—an Absolutely Absurd Ape (Eric Carle, 1974)
Dr. Seuss's ABC (Dr. Seuss, Random House, 1963)
The Biggest Tongue Twister Book in the World (Gyles Brandeth, Sterling, l978)
Alphabet Annie Announces an All-American Album (Susan Purviance and
Marcia O'Shell, Houghton Mifflin, 1988)
A Twister of Twists, A Tangler of Tongues and *Busy Buzzing Bumblebees
and Other Tongue Twisters* (Alvin Schwartz, Harper Collins, 1972)
Six Sick Sheep (Jan Cole, Morrow, 1993)
Animalia (Graeme Base, Abrams, 1987)

Roger Rabbit runs relays.
Susie's sister sipped seven sodas.
Tom took ten turtles to town.
Veronica visited very vicious volcanoes.
Wild Willy went west.
Yippy yanked Yolanda's yellow yoyo.
Zany Zeb zapped Zeke's zebra.

As you work with books with lots of words that begin the same and tongue twisters, begin by emphasizing the words that start the same. This is the phonemic awareness understanding that underlies phonics knowledge. When your children can tell you whether or not words start with the same sound and can come up with other words that start that way, shift your instruction to which letter makes which sound. You can use the very same books and tongue twisters again, this time emphasizing the sound of the letter. Books with alliteration and tongue twisters can help your children develop the "starts the same" component of phonemic awareness and can help them learn some letter sounds.

Sound Boxes

Some children find it very difficult to segment words into sounds. Many teachers have found success using a technique called sound boxes (Elkonin, 1973), in which children push chips, pennies, or other objects into boxes as they hear the sounds. In the first lessons, children have a drawing of three boxes.

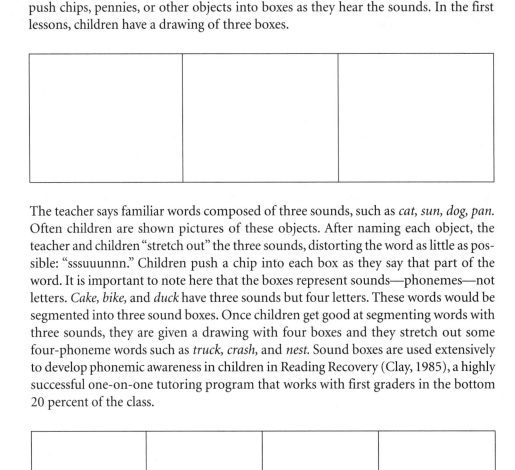

The teacher says familiar words composed of three sounds, such as *cat, sun, dog, pan.* Often children are shown pictures of these objects. After naming each object, the teacher and children "stretch out" the three sounds, distorting the word as little as possible: "sssuuunnn." Children push a chip into each box as they say that part of the word. It is important to note here that the boxes represent sounds—phonemes—not letters. *Cake, bike,* and *duck* have three sounds but four letters. These words would be segmented into three sound boxes. Once children get good at segmenting words with three sounds, they are given a drawing with four boxes and they stretch out some four-phoneme words such as *truck, crash,* and *nest.* Sound boxes are used extensively to develop phonemic awareness in children in Reading Recovery (Clay, 1985), a highly successful one-on-one tutoring program that works with first graders in the bottom 20 percent of the class.

Once children can push the chips to represent sounds, they can push letter cards into boxes. From the letters *m, b, s, t,* and *a,* the teacher could ask the children to push these letters to spell words such as *sat, bat, mat, bam, Sam, tab, bats, mats, tabs,* and *stab.* Children should not work with letters in the sound boxes until they have developed some phonemic awareness and are working on learning letter names and letter sounds. Later on, children can actually write the letters in the boxes as they are attempting to spell words they are writing.

Use Names to Build Phonological and Phonemic Awareness

You can use your children's names to build phonological and phonemic awareness.

Clap Syllables The first way that children learn to pull apart words is into syllables. Say each child's name and have the children clap the beats in that name as they say it with you. Help children to see that Tran and Pat are one-beat names, Manuel and Patrick, two beats, and so on. Once children begin to understand, clap the beats and have all the children whose names have that number of beats stand up and say their names as they clap the beats with you.

Matching Beginning Sounds Say a sound—not a letter name—and have all the children whose names begin with that sound come forward. Stretch out the sound as you make it: "ssss." For the "sss" sound, Samantha, Susie, Steve, and Cynthia should all come forward. Have everyone stretch out the "sss" as they say the names. If anyone points out that Cynthia starts with a *c* or that Sharon starts with an *s,* explain that they are correct about the letters but that now you are listening for sounds.

Hear Rhyming Words Choose the children whose names have lots of rhyming words to come forward. Say a word that rhymes with one of the names and have the children say the word along with the name of the rhyming child.

Segment Words into Sounds Call children to line up by stretching out their names, emphasizing each letter. As each child lines up, have the class stretch out the name with you.

Summary

Phonological and phonemic awareness is an essential part of the foundation for learning to read. Children need to understand how sounds go together in words. They need to be able to manipulate words in their heads. The activities in this chapter mimic activities children from literacy-rich homes do before coming to school. If schools provide young children with a variety of activities such as those suggested here, all children can develop phonological and phonemic awareness and greatly increase the possibility that they will become fluent readers and writers.

chapter 4

Concrete Words, Letter Names, and Sounds

In addition to print concepts and phonological and phonemic awareness, the foundation for success in learning to read and write requires that children learn some concrete words, letter names, and sounds. If children have been engaging in the activities described in the previous three chapters, most children will have already begun developing these skills. Activities in this chapter build on and extend the activities from previous chapters to help all children learn some concrete words, letter names, and sounds.

 ## Names

In Chapter Two, you learned how to do the Getting to Know You activity to help children get off to a successful start in reading and to build print concepts. In addition to writing and reading charts about each child, most teachers also focus activities on each child's name.

As described in Chapter One, children need to learn some concrete words—interesting, important-to-them words. Names are often the first words many children learn to read, and they are immensely interested in their name and the names of their friends.

We create a name board to display the names, often with photos of each child. Each day a name is pulled and everyone's attention is focused on that name. After doing the activities with each child's name, the name is added to the name board. Here are some of the activities we do with the names.

The First Name

Reach into your container and pull out a name. Assume that David is the first name to come out. Point to the word *David* on the sentence strip and develop children's understanding of jargon by pointing out that this word is David's name. Tell them that it takes many letters to write the word *David* and let them help you count the letters. Say the letters in *David*—*D-a-v-i-d*—and have the children chant them with you cheerleader style. (We call this cheering for David and he loves it!) Point out that the word *David* begins and ends with the same letter. Explain that the *d* looks different because one is a capital *D* and the other is a small *d*—or uppercase and lowercase— whatever jargon you use.

Take another sentence strip and have children watch as you write *David*. Have them chant the spelling of the letters with you. Cut the letters apart and mix them up. Let several children come and arrange the letters in just the right order so that they spell *David*. Have the other children chant to check that the order is correct. Display David's name on a bulletin board reserved for the names. Include a photo of David if possible.

The Next Names

Imagine that it is the next day and the name pulled from the box is Catherine. Hold up the sentence strip and have the children say the letters in *Catherine* with you. Next, have the children chant the letters—cheering for Catherine. Help the children count the letters and decide which letter is first, last, and so on. Point out that *Catherine* has two *e*'s and they look exactly the same because they are both small (lowercase) *e*'s. Write *Catherine* on another sentence strip and cut it into letters. Have children arrange the letters to spell *Catherine*, using the first sentence strip name as their model.

Put *Catherine* on the name board and compare the two names. Which has the most letters? How many more letters are in the word *Catherine* than in the word *David*? Does *Catherine* have any of the same letters as *David*?

The next name to come out is *Robert*. Do all the same activities for Robert. Say and count the letters. Cheer for Robert by chanting the letters in his name. Write his name again, cutting it into letters and rearranging the letters to spell his name. Be sure to note the two *r*'s and talk about why they look different.

As you put *Robert* on the name board, compare it to both *David* and *Catherine*. *Robert* has an *e* and *Catherine* has two *e*'s. *Robert* and *Catherine* both have a *t*. *Robert* doesn't have any of the same letters that *David* has. Robert's name has six letters—more than *David* but less than *Catherine*.

Mike comes out next. When you have a one-syllable name with which there are many rhymes (*Pat, Tran, Joe, Sue*, etc.), seize the opportunity to help the children listen for words that rhyme with that name. Say pairs of words—some of which rhyme with Mike:

Mike/ball   Mike/bike   Mike/hike   Mike/cook   Mike/like

If the pairs rhyme, everyone should point at Mike and whisper, "Mike." If not, they should shake their heads and frown.

Cindy comes out. *Catherine* and *Cindy* both begin with the letter *c* but begin with different sounds. Have Catherine and Cindy stand on opposite sides of you. Write their names above them on the chalkboard. Have the children say *Catherine* and *Cindy* several times—drawing out the first sound. Help them to understand that some letters can have more than one sound and that the names *Catherine* and *Cindy* show us that. Tell the class that you are going to say some words, all of which begin with the letter *c*. Some of these words sound like *Catherine* at the beginning and some of them sound like *Cindy*. Say some words and have the children say them with you:

cat   celery   candy   cookies   city   cereal   cut

For each word, have them point to Catherine or Cindy to show which sound they hear. Once they have decided, write each word under *Catherine* or *Cindy*.

Continue to pull names each day and as you add each to your board or wall, help the children notice whatever they can about letter–sound relationships. The names your children have will determine what you will help the children to notice. If you don't have names such as *Catherine* and *Cindy*, you would not point out the two sounds of *c* this early in the year but, if you do, you have to help the children understand that some letters have more than one sound or they will get confused. Children do notice things we don't point out and if we just teach *c* as having the sound in *Catherine, cat,* and *candy,* Cindy may be looking at her nametag and wondering why she can't hear the sound! English is not a one-letter, one-sound language. There are relationships but they are complex. We must help children see how letters represent sounds, but if we make it simpler than it really is, some children are apt to notice the contradiction and get confused and maybe come to the dangerous conclusion that "there isn't any system and pattern to these letters and sounds."

So, if you have a *Joseph* and a *Julio* or a *Sheila* and a *Sam,* use the preceding procedure when the second name goes up. Point out that it is the *sh* in *Sheila* that gives *s* its different sound. Most of the children who are just beginning to learn about how letters and sounds are related would not need to know this. But those who were already reading when they came to first grade probably know the single-letter sounds and are ready to realize that some letter combinations have different sounds.

Finally, as you get to about the halfway point in adding the names, let the children take charge of noticing the similarities and differences between the names. Instead of pointing out as you add *Rasheed* that his name starts with the same letter and sound as *Robert* and he has two *e*'s and his name ends with a *d* like *David*, ask the children:

> "What do you notice about the letters and sounds in Rasheed's name and the other names on the board?"

There are a system and a pattern to the way letters in English represent sounds. Our instruction should point out these patterns. Children who see a new word and ask themselves how that new word is like the other words they know can discover many patterns on their own.

When All the Names Are Displayed

Once all the names are displayed and most children have learned most of the names, we can begin to solidify some of that letter–name sound knowledge. Imagine that the names of our children displayed on the word wall or name board are:

David	Rasheed	Robert	Catherine	Cindy
Mike	Sheila	Sam	Joseph	Julio
Amber T.	Matt	Erin	Shawonda	Bianca
Erica	Kevin	Adam	Delano	Brittany
Bo	Tara	Amber M.	Octavius	Kelsie

Begin with a letter that many children have in their names and that usually has its expected sound. With this class you might begin with the letter *r*. Have all children whose names have an *r* in them come to the front of the class, holding a card with their names on it. First count all the *r*'s. There are nine *r*'s in all. Next have the children whose name contains an *r* divide themselves into those whose names begin with an *r*—Robert and Rasheed; those whose names end with an *r*—Amber T. and Amber M.; and those with an *r* that is not the first or the last letter—Brittany, Erica, Tara, Erin, Catherine. Finally, say each name slowly—stretching out the letters—and decide if you can hear the usual sound of that letter. For *r*, you can hear them all.

Now choose another letter and let all those children come down and display their name cards. Count the number of times that letter occurs and then have the children divide themselves into groups according to whether the letter is first, last, or in between. Finally, say the names stretching them out and decide if you can hear the usual sound that letter makes. *D* would be a good second choice. You would have David and Delano beginning with *d;* David and Rasheed ending with *d;* Cindy, Shawonda, and Adam having a *d* that is not first or last. Again, you can hear the usual sound of *d* in all these names.

Continue picking letters and having children come up with their name cards until you have sorted for some of the letters represented by your names. When doing the letters *s, c, t,* and *j,* be sure to point out that they can have two sounds and that the *th* in *Catherine* and the *sh* in *Sheila, Shawonda,* and *Rasheed* have their own special sounds. You probably wouldn't sort out the names with an *h* because although *Shawanda, Sheila, Rasheed, Catherine,* and *Joseph* have an *h,* the *h* sound is not represented by any of these. The same would go for the *p,* which only occurs in *Joseph.* When you have the children come down for the vowels, *a, e, i, o,* and *u,* count and then sort the children according to first, last, and in between but do not try to listen for the sounds. Explain that vowels have lots of different sounds and that they will learn more about the vowels and their sounds throughout the year.

 # Alphabet Books

The Alphabet Song has been sung by generations of children. Children enjoy it, and it does seem to give them a sense of all the letters and a framework in which to put new letters as they learn them. Many children come to school already able to sing *The Alphabet Song.* Let them sing it and let them teach it to everyone else. Once the children can sing the song, you may want to point to alphabet cards (usually found above the chalkboard) as they sing. Children enjoy "being the alphabet" as they line up to go somewhere. Simply pass out laminated alphabet cards—one to each child, leftovers to the teacher—and let the children sing the song slowly as each child lines up. Be sure to hand out the cards randomly so that no one gets to be the *A* and lead the line or has to be the *Z* and bring up the rear every day!

There are also lots of wonderful alphabet books to read and enjoy. Many of these fit into your themes or units. Research shows that simple books with not too many words on a page and pictures that most of the children recognize are the most helpful to children in building their letter–sound and letter–name knowledge. Once the book has been read and reread several times, children will enjoy reading it during their self-selected reading time. It is very important that children have time to choose and read books each day. Simple alphabet books that have been read to the class provide books that children can read on their own before they can read books with more text.

There are too many wonderful alphabet books to name them all here, but a few just have to be mentioned. *The Peek-a-Boo ABC* has little doors that you open. Inside the door to the barn is a bear. A clown appears as you open the door to the car, and lions can be found in the lunchbox. When reading this one with children for the second or third time, we pause before opening each door to see if they remember that it is salami in the sandwich and a watermelon in the whale. Another alphabet book the children adore is the *A to Z Sticker Book.* Each page has three or four pictures along with the words and one word with no picture. On the *d* page, you see the words *donkey, dinosaur,* and *dolphins* along with pictures of these. The word *drum* has a space next to it, and you have to find the sticker on the sticker pages in the middle to go with it. Stickers peel off and go back to their spots when the book is read so that the whole process can be done again and again.

Once you and the children have read several alphabet books, you might want to make a class alphabet book and/or have each child make one. Work on a few pages each day and use all your resources—alphabet books you read to them, things in the room, places children like to eat—to brainstorm a huge list of the possible words for each page. Depending on your class, you may want to put just one word and picture on each page or several words and pictures for each letter. If children are making individual

Alphabet Books

Here are a few alphabet books that meet our "not too many words, familiar pictures, kids love to read them" criteria:

The Peek-a-Boo ABC (Demi, Random House, 1982)
A to Z Sticker Book (Jan Pienkowski, Random House, 1995)
It Begins with an A (Stephanie Calmenson, Hyperion, 1993)
Alphabet Puzzle (Jill Downie, Lothrop, 1988)
Dr. Seuss's ABC (Dr. Seuss, Random House, 1963)
The Alphabet Tale (Jan Garten, Random House, 1964)
Easy as Pie (Marcia and Michael Folsom, Houghton Mifflin, 1986)
Eating the Alphabet (Lois Ehlert, Harcourt, 1989)
By the Sea: An Alphabet Book (Ann Blades, Kids Can Press, 1985)
The Accidental Zucchini (Max Grover, Harcourt, 1993)
NBA Action from A to Z (James Preller, Scholastic, 1997)
The Timbertoes ABC Alphabet Book (Highlights for Children, Boyds Mill Press, 1997)
A Is for Astronaut (Stan Tucker, Simon & Schuster, 1995)
Paddington's ABC (Michael Bond, Puffin Books, 1996)
John Burmingham's ABC (John Burmingham, Crown, 1993)
Alphababies (Kim Golding, DK Publishing, 1998)
The Monster Book of ABC Sounds (Alan Snow, Puffin, 1994)

books, let them choose the order in which they will select the letters for the books as well as the words for their pages. They will most often choose the letters they know best first. Knowing what they choose can help teachers identify what it is that children know.

Letter Actions and Foods

Eating and actions are important activities to young children. Teaching children actions for the consonant letters and having them associate these letters with foods help some children remember their sounds. For each action, write the letter on one side of a large index card and the action on the other. The first time you teach each letter, make a big deal of it. Get out the rhythm sticks and the marching music when you march. Go out on the playground and jump rope and do jumping jacks. Play hopscotch and pretend to be bunnies when you introduce *h*.

Once the children have learned actions for several letters, there are many activities you can do right in the classroom without any props. Have all the children stand by their desks and wait until you show them a letter. They should do that action until you hide that letter behind your back. When they have all stopped and you have their attention again, show them another letter and have them do that action. Continue this with as many letters as you have time to fill. Be sure to make comments, such as, "Yes, I see everyone marching because *m* is our marching letter."

In another activity, you pass out the letters for which children have learned actions to individual children. Each child gets up and does the action required and calls on someone to guess which letter that child was given.

In Follow the Letter Leader, the leader picks a letter card and does that action. Everyone else follows the leader doing the same action. The leader then picks another card, and the game continues.

Teachers have different favorite actions, and you will have your own favorites. Try to pick actions with which everyone is familiar and that are called by only one name. Here is a list of actions I like. The action for *s* is my particular favorite. You can use it to end the game. Children say, "It is not an action at all," but they remember that "*s* is the sitting letter":

bounce	hop	nod	vacuum
catch	jump	paint	walk
dance	kick	run	yawn
fall	laugh	sit	zip
gallop	march	talk	

Children remember what they do and what they eat. Many teachers like to feature a food for each letter. Children help to prepare the food and then eat it. Try to pick nutritious foods that children like, although even the children who hated zucchini remembered it was their *z* food! When they complained, their teacher asked, "What food do you like that begins with *z*?" Later, a child brought zucchini bread, which was a hit with most. Some possible foods:

bananas	hamburgers	noodles	vegetables
cookies	Jell-O	pizza	watermelon
donuts	Kool-Aid	raisins	yogurt
fish	lemonade	soup	zucchini bread
gum	milk	toast	

Key Words for Sounds

Once your children are moving along in their phonemic awareness, have learned many of the letter names, and are beginning to learn some of the sounds, you can help them consolidate this knowledge by deciding with them on one key word to represent each sound. Many publishing companies and reading series include some key words for the common letter sounds, but often children call the word something other than what is intended ("puppy" for *dog* or "bunny" for *rabbit,* for example), and the key words can confuse rather than support their learning of letter sounds. Many teachers work with their classes to come up with a key word that works for them. Let all the children have a say in this and spend some time discussing which word would be most helpful and which word they like best. Remember that "liking something" is very important to young children! You may want to use some of the wonderful examples from alphabet books, some of the names of your children when they are clear examples for the

The Series

Alphabet Starters (Rigby, 1996) provides little books for each letter of the alphabet. Each book contains seven key words with wonderfully clear pictures. The *g* book has words and pictures for *gate, girls, goats, garage, garden, goggles,* and *guitar.* The *r* book has *rabbit, red, road, river, rainbow, ring,* and *rope.* Books for the vowels have pictures and words for both the long and short sounds. The *i* book has *insects, invitation, igloo, ice cream,* and an *iron.* Young children love reading these simple but engaging books, and the books help them learn letter sounds along with the important phonemic awareness concept of "starts the same."

sound, and some favorite foods and favorite places familiar to all your children. For the vowels, you may want two examples, one for each of the common sounds. Try to use "pure" sounds—a word with just *f*, not *fr* or *fl*—since separating these blended sounds is difficult for children in the beginning. Here are the key words one class decided they liked. The names are all names of children in the class or of famous people. Use this as an example of the kind of chart your children might help construct, but remember this only works if the children have ownership in choosing the words and if they like their choices.

A a	apple, ape		N n	nose
B b	boys		O o	octopus, Oprah
C c	cookies		P p	Pizza Hut
D d	dinosaur		Q u	quarter
E e	elephant, Ethan		R r	red
F f	fun		S s	soup
G g	girls		T t	Taco Bell
H h	Hardees		U u	underwear, unicorn
I i	insect, ice cream		V v	Vicki
J j	Jessica		W w	Wendy's
K k	Kmart		X x	x-ray
L l	Latecia		Y y	yellow
M m	McDonald's		Z z	zoo

Changing a Hen to a Fox

Children love to pretend, and in this activity they pretend they can change one animal, a hen, into a fox. They do this by changing one letter at a time. As they change that letter, they listen for where they hear the changing letter and review all the single consonants. To begin this activity, we write the names of five animals on the board—each of which has a different vowel sound:

cat   hen   pig   fox   bug

The teacher and the children say these words together, stretching out each word and talking about the beginning, middle, and ending sounds. Particular attention is given to the middle sound—the vowel sound—in each of these words. Next the teacher asks the children,

"Can you change a hen into a fox?"

She tells the children that if they follow her directions and think about letters and sounds, they will be able do this. The children all take a sheet of paper and these directions are given.

"Write *hen*." (The teacher points to the word *hen* on the board and everyone copies it onto their papers.)

"Now change the hen to *pen*." (The teacher and children decide they have to change just the first letter from an *h* to a *p* and write *pen* under *hen*.)

"Now change your pen into a *pet*." (Children decide they have to change the last letter from an *n* to a *t* and write *pet*.)

"Can you change pet to *pit*?" (The teacher helps them stretch out *pit* and decide it is the vowel they need to change and this vowel has the same sound as *pig*.)

"Now change pit to *sit*."

"Next change sit to *six*."

"Then change six to *fix*."

"Finally, change fix to *fox*."

Children love changing the letters and the animals, and they are using what they are learning about letters and sounds to spell lots of other words. (Many teachers initiate this activity by reading Mem Fox's *Hattie and the Fox* to the children.)

Here are seven other Changing a Hen to a Fox lessons.

pig	bug	pig	cat	fox	bug	cat
rig	dug	big	bat	box	hug	hat
rid	dig	wig	hat	bop	dug	rat
rib	pig	win	rat	top	dig	rag
rob	pin	fin	pat	mop	big	bag
Bob	pen	fit	pet	map	bag	big
box	ten	fat	pen	mat	bat	dig
fox	hen	cat	hen	cat	cat	pig

Guess the Covered Word

Most short words are made up of two patterns, the beginning letters and the vowel and letters that follow it. The beginning letters (which linguists call onsets and educators call consonants, digraphs, and blends or clusters) are all the letters up to the vowel. Children need to learn the sounds for these letters—which are quite consistent and reliable. Unfortunately, although many children "learn" these sounds—they can circle pictures that begin with them and tell you what letter makes a particular sound if you ask them—they don't use them when they read and write. When writing and trying to figure out the spelling of a word such as *smelly*, they might begin it just with an *s* or an *sl* instead of an *sm*. Faced with an unfamiliar word in their reading, they often guess a word that makes sense but does not begin with the right letters or guess a word with only the correct first letter, ignoring the other letters. All of the activities in this chapter stress learning and using all the beginning letters. Guess the Covered Word lessons teach these beginning letter sounds systematically and teach them in the context of reading. Children learn that guessing just based on beginning letters—or just based on making sense—is not a very good strategy. But when you use all the beginning letters and the sense of the sentence and consider the length of the word, you can make very good guesses at new words.

Here are the beginning letters children need to learn to use. We are using the jargon here—consonants, digraphs, and so on—so that you will recognize what is being taught, but we avoid it "like the plague" with children who get so confused by all the terms that they can't focus on what we want them to—learning and using the sounds of the letters. We teach children the sounds for, and to look and listen for, "all the beginning letters—all the letters up to the vowel."

Single consonants: *b c d f g h j k l m n p r s t v w y z* (including the "s" sound of *c* in *city* and the "j" sound of *g* in *gym*)

Digraphs (two letters, one sound): *sh ch wh th*

Other two-letter, one-sound combinations: *ph wr kn qu*

Blends (beginning letters blended together, sometimes called clusters): *bl br cl cr dr fl fr gl gr pl pr sc scr sk sl sm sn sp spr st str sw tr*

This chart is ready for a Guess the Covered Word lesson.

Guess the Covered Word lessons help students learn to cross-check—to simultaneously think about what would make sense and about letters and sounds. To prepare for a Guess the Covered Word activity, we write 5–7 sentences on the board and cover one word in each sentence. We use sticky notes to cover the words and cover them in such a way that, after three or four guesses are made with no letters showing, we can uncover all the letters up to the vowel. For our first lessons, the sentences follow a similar word pattern: We cover the final word, and we include in our covered words only words that begin with a single initial consonant.

Kevin wants a pet <u>hamster</u>.
Mike wants a pet <u>python</u>.
Paola wants a pet <u>goldfish</u>.
Ryan wants a pet <u>turtle</u>.
Devon wants a pet <u>pony</u>.
Jasmine wants a pet <u>kitten</u>.

We begin the activity by reading the first sentence and asking students to guess the covered word. We write three or four guesses next to the sentence. Pointing out to the children that "it sure can be a lot of words when you can't see any letters," we uncover all the letters up to the vowel (which in these first lessons is only one). We erase guesses that don't begin with that letter and have students suggest possible words that make sense and begin with the correct letter and write these responses. When all the guesses that begin correctly and make sense are written, we uncover the whole word and go on to the next sentence.

Some teachers use the overhead for Guess the Covered Word lessons.

We use Guess the Covered Word activities to teach and review all the beginning sounds. As the children begin to understand the strategy they need to use, we don't limit the covered word to the final position. Now they read the whole sentence, skipping the covered word and then coming back to it to make guesses. We follow the same procedure of getting three or four guesses with no letters showing and then uncovering all the letters up to the vowel. Here are some sentences we might use when we are focusing on the digraphs *sh, ch, wh,* and *th.*

Corinda likes to eat <u>chicken</u>.
Chad ate <u>thirteen</u> waffles.
Sean likes orange <u>sherbet</u>.
Bob likes strawberry <u>shortcake</u>.
Chris bakes pies for <u>Thanksgiving</u>.
Carol likes chocolate <u>cake</u>.

We teach and practice all the blends with Guess the Covered Word activities:

> We all love it when it <u>snows</u>.
> Some people go <u>skiing</u>.
> People ride in <u>snowmobiles</u>.
> The <u>snowplow</u> is fun to ride on, too!
> You can go down a hill fast in a <u>sled</u>.
> Walking back up is hard if the snow is <u>slippery</u>.

Guess the Covered Word is a very versatile strategy. We sometimes use Big Books and cover a word or two on each page. We also write paragraphs summarizing what we have learned during a science or social studies unit and cover words in it.

Through Guess the Covered Word activities, children learn that just guessing words is not a good decoding strategy, but when you guess something that makes sense in the sentence, has all the right letters up to the vowel (not just the first one), and is the right length, you can figure out many new words.

Summary: How the Foundational Activities Are Multilevel

All the activities for building the foundation have "something for everyone." Regardless of where your students are in their phonics and spelling abilities, there are things they can learn from each lesson format.

During shared reading with predictable books, predictable chart, and writing activities, children learn what they are ready to learn. Children with little print experience learn what reading is and begin to develop "concepts of print." They learn that each sentence starts at the left and goes to the right. They see the teacher start at the top and go the bottom. They hear the teacher talk about "words," "sentences," and "letters" and learn what this print-related jargon means. Most children learn a few words and begin to notice how words are the same and different. Children who come to school with these print concepts already established are not "spinning their wheels." These children actually learn many of the words in the books and charts. Often they can read these books and charts entirely on their own. Perhaps most important, all children develop the desire to learn to read and the confidence that they *are* learning to read!

Getting to Know You is a multilevel activity in which there are multiple things to be learned and multiple ways for children to move forward. After participating in the interviewing, shared writing, name board activities, and focusing on each child's name, children who enter with almost no understanding of what reading and writing are learn print concepts, some concrete words, and some letter names and sounds. More advanced children can read everyone's charts and know most of the words on these charts!

All the activities with rhyme and with the alphabet develop phonemic awareness skills. They also allow children who have well-developed phonemic awareness to learn letter names and sounds that move them forward in their reading.

Changing a Hen to a Fox provides practice with beginning, middle (vowel), and ending sounds. Children develop their phonemic awareness as they stretch out words and hear where in the word the letter needs to be changed. Children who know letter sounds see how these help them to spell lots of words.

Guess the Covered Word lessons provide continuous practice with all the beginning letter patterns. Children who already know most of their beginning letter sounds learn the important strategy of using meaning, all the beginning letters, and word length as cues to the identification of an unknown word.

In classroom after classroom, children who enter school naive about literacy and who participate in the foundational activities develop those abilities and concepts essential for success in learning to read. More important for the long haul, these children all see themselves as readers and writers and maintain their "of course, I can" attitude.

While these children are developing the critical foundation for moving into literacy, other children who come prepared but not reading are actually learning to read and write. These children can read and write the names of almost all their classmates. They can name all the letters that occur in these names and have begun looking for patterns and relationships between letters and sounds. All of these children can read the chart articles about themselves and most can read a lot of the words in the articles about the whole class. Most of the children have learned to read many high-frequency words (*the, in, he, she, boy, girl, likes,* etc.) that occur over and over in the charts and predictable books.

All these activities are multilevel—they have different things you can learn from them depending on where you are. Children who come in ahead will continue to move ahead as children lacking print experiences build the necessary foundation.

part two

Fluency

Fluency is the ability to read most words in context quickly, accurately, automatically, and with appropriate expression. Fluency is critical to reading comprehension because of the attention factor. Part Two has two chapters that provide activities for helping children learn to read and write fluently.

Chapter Five defines fluency and suggests classroom-tested ways to develop fluency. Children become fluent readers as they engage in lots of independent reading, write daily, and participate in some repeated reading activities. A Fluency Development Lesson that can be easily included in any teaching setting is described.

Chapter Six describes activities for teaching high-frequency words. In English, a little over 100 words account for every other word we read and write. Most of these words are abstract, meaningless, connecting words. Many of them have irregular spellings and pronunciations. Chapter Six describes ways to build meaning for these words and explains how to use a word wall so that children learn to automatically and rapidly identify these words while reading and spell them while writing. Chapter Six ends with an explanation of how all the fluency and word-wall activities are multilevel.

Fluency Activities

luency is the ability to read most words in context quickly, accurately, automatically, and with appropriate expression. Fluency is critical to reading comprehension because of the attention factor. Our brains can attend to only a limited number of things at a time. If most of our attention is focused on decoding the words, there is little attention left for the comprehension part of reading—putting the words together and thinking about what they mean. The National Reading Panel (2000) explains this relationship between reading comprehension and fluency:

> If text is read in a laborious and inefficient manner, it will
> be difficult for the child to remember what has been read
> and to relate the ideas expressed in the text to his or her
> background knowledge. (p. 11)

Fluency is not something a reader has or doesn't have. In fact, how fluent a reader you are is directly related to the complexity of the text you are reading. If you are reading a text with lots of words you have read accurately many times before, you probably recognize those familiar words immediately and automatically. All your attention is then available to think about the meaning of what you are reading. If you are reading a text with lots of words you have never encountered in print before, you will have to stop and decode these words in some way—using the letter–sound and morphemic patterns you know to turn the printed letters into sounds and words. In order to comprehend what you have decoded, you may have to reread the text once or even twice so that your attention is freed from decoding and available for comprehending.

When you are reading or writing, your brain is busy constructing meaning and is simultaneously identifying or spelling words. Most of the time, you don't even know that you are identifying or spelling words because you have read or written these words so many times that their identification and spelling have become "automatic." *Automatic* means without any conscious effort or thought. The concept of automaticity is critical to your understanding of the word/meaning construction relationship because your brain can carry out many automatic functions simultaneously (perhaps you have some background music on right now and are listening automatically as you identify words automatically too), but the brain can do only one nonautomatic function. Meaning construction is the nonautomatic function. When your brain is stopped by a word you can't immediately and automatically identify or spell, the brain's attention is diverted from meaning to words. In order to read and write fluently, readers and writers must be able to immediately recognize and spell the vast majority of the words.

Fluency is fast, expressive reading. The easiest way to imagine fluency is to remember what a nonfluent reader sounds like:

> Some children read one word at a time hes—si—ta—ting and and and re—peat—ing words.

In the previous sentence, I have tried to remind you what a nonfluent reader sounds like. Every teacher has had the experience of working with children who can read most words but for whom reading is a tortured, labored word-by-word, sometimes syllable-by-syllable, process. Nonfluent reading is slow, labored, and lacking in expression and phrasing. Fluency is the ability to quickly and automatically identify the words. Fluent reading is not saying one word at a time. Fluent reading puts words together in phrases and has the expression you would use if you were speaking the words.

Children become fluent readers by reading and rereading lots of easy books. Most children who have favorite books at home in their own personal libraries read these books over and over. This rereading of favorite books contributes greatly to the development of fluency and teachers of beginning readers need to provide time for children to read and reread favorite books as part of the school day.

Fluency is also important for writing. When you are writing, you have many things to think about, including what you want to say, how to begin, what the best words are, and when you are at the end of a sentence what kind of punctuation that sentence needs. These and many other decisions vie for the attention of every writer. Writers also have to decide how to spell the words they have chosen to represent the

Fluency and Rate Increase across the Grade Levels

The average first grader by the end of first grade when reading material at first-grade level reads about 60–90 words per minute (wpm). Average reading rates increase across grade levels and are estimated at:

Grade 1 =   60–90 wpm
Grade 2 =   85–120 wpm
Grade 3 = 115–140 wpm
Grade 4 = 140–170 wpm
Adult   = 250–300 wpm

Source: Estimates from Harris and Sipay (1990).

ideas they want to convey. For young writers, spelling takes a lot of their attention. Any attention or energy devoted to thinking about how to spell words takes attention away from all the other things writers must juggle. Being able to automatically spell high-frequency words is as important to fluent writing as being able to instantly recognize these words is to fluent reading.

The classroom that helps all children develop fluency is one in which there is attention to high-frequency words, many and varied opportunities for rereading, and lots of reading and writing throughout the school day.

Independent Reading Develops Fluency

Independent reading is a critical daily component of a balanced reading program in any classroom. Some significant amount of time every day in every classroom should be devoted to children choosing for themselves something to read and then settling down to read it. Independent reading is often promoted in terms of the motivation and interest children develop as they have time to pursue their own personal interests through books. In addition, the amount of reading children do is the biggest variable in their word fluency, and children who engage in regular self-selected reading read a lot more than children who don't.

All a teacher of young children has to do to have a successful self-selected reading program is to provide a good reading model through daily teacher–read aloud, schedule time each day for children to read books they choose, and provide lots of different books on all different levels and of all different types. For older children—particularly children who are not fluent readers—it is not so easy. These nonfluent older readers don't think of themselves as good readers and don't want to read the easy books they deem "baby books!"

Linda Fielding and Cathy Roller attack this "baby book attitude" head on in a 1992 *Reading Teacher* article, "Making Difficult Books Accessible and Easy Books Acceptable." Among the ideas for making difficult books accessible are:

1. Provide independent reading time when children can self-select books (including nonfiction) and interact with others about what they learn from these books.

2. If books are too difficult for most children to read, read these aloud to them.

3. Partner the children, putting a more able reader with a less able reader.

4. Provide lots of rereading opportunities because difficult material becomes easier each time it is read.

5. Precede difficult books on a topic with easier books on that topic to build background knowledge.

All these suggestions will help children read with more fluency even when the material they are reading is more difficult than it should optimally be.

Among their many practical ideas for making easy books acceptable, Fielding and Roller suggest:

1. Modeling, by reading aloud, the use and enjoyment of easy books.

2. Altering purposes for easy reading by having older children read these books to younger buddies.

3. Allowing children to make tape recordings of favorite books.

4. Making the expanding world of nonfiction books readily available.

I have seen all four of these strategies successfully used and even a combination that worked like this. A fourth-grade teacher with many children still reading—not very fluently—at first- and second-grade levels decided that the children needed to do lots of easy reading. She partnered each child with a kindergartner and arranged for a weekly reading time. She then gathered up a lot of easy books, including many Dr. Seuss titles, Clifford books, and many nonfiction picture books (including alphabet books, some of which are listed in Chapter Four). Across the course of a week or two, she read these books to her children and let each child choose one book to prepare to read to the kindergarten buddy. When the children had chosen their books, they practiced reading the book several times—with a partner—to the tape recorder and finally to the teacher. By the time her children trotted down to the kindergarten—easy books proudly in hand—all the children were fluent readers of their book.

Upon their return to the fourth grade, they talked about their experience with their kindergarten buddies and whether or not their book was a good choice. The teacher made a chart on which each child listed the book read aloud that week. The following day, the teacher and the children gathered and reviewed the chart showing who had read what. The teacher also reminded them of some other books no one had chosen the first week and led them to choose their second book. The partner reading, tape-recorder reading, and reading to the teacher continued as it had for the first week except that, if a child chose a book that another child had read the previous week, that child became the "expert" on that book and read the book to or listened to the new reader read the book at least once. The second trip to the kindergarten went more smoothly than the first, and the children returned, discussed the kindergartners' responses to the books, and listed the second book they had read on the chart.

By the fourth week, the easy-reading-for-fluency program was up and running with minimal help from the teacher. Many children chose books their friends had chosen previously, and they enjoyed reading together and often tape recording the book together in preparation for performing their weekly "civic volunteer" duty!

Daily Writing Develops Fluency

In addition to lots of reading, lots of writing helps children become better decoders and spellers. This is especially true when young children are encouraged to invent-spell the words they need but haven't yet learned to spell. Clarke (1988) compared the decoding ability of end-of-the-year first graders and found that first graders who had been encouraged to invent-spell in first grade were better at decoding words than first graders from classrooms that emphasized correct spelling. One of the biggest concerns teachers express as they teach young children about sound and letter patterns is that the children don't apply what they know to actually figuring out words while reading. To invent-spell a word, however, you have to apply what you know because using your letter–sound knowledge is the way you get some letters to represent the word.

There are some words we don't want children to invent-spell. High-frequency words such as *they, said,* and *from* are often spelled in the logical—but incorrect way— "thay, sed, frum." Chapter Six will describe how to use a Word Wall to teach high-frequency words. When children write, they spell words as best they can in first draft—unless it is on the word wall. Word-wall words must be spelled correctly in everything children write because once you do something over and over again, it becomes automatic. Children who write without a high-frequency word wall may write "thay, sed, frum" thousands of time and they will become automatic at spelling these words incorrectly.

Establishing a daily writing time is not difficult with young children. They all have things they want to tell, and if teachers model writing during a minilesson, encourage children to write about what they want to write about, and accept whatever writing they can do, young children delight in writing!

Older, struggling nonfluent readers do not delight in writing. In fact, they will tell you they hate to write. This "I hate to write" attitude can be turned around—but it takes patience and determination.

If you teach older nonfluent readers, you must first convince yourself of the value of their writing. As they write and spell the word-wall words correctly, they will become much faster and fluent at writing these words. As they "stretch out" some words to put down what they want to tell, they will be applying what they are learning about letter patterns and decoding. The more and faster they can write, the better they will like it!

Writing promotes word fluency. If you teach older children who hate to write, start doing a word wall and some of the activities described in the next chapter. Then schedule daily, short—10 minutes maximum—writing times. Model how to write by letting children watch you writing a few sentences about something you want to tell them, thinking aloud as you write. After they write, let them share if they choose to by reading or telling what they have written. Let them choose what they want to write about and emphasize that you are interested in what they want to tell and, as long as they spell word-wall words correctly, they should spell the other words as best they can.

Don't worry about publishing or what the final product looks like until your students get over their "I hate to write" attitudes. Then you can begin to help them improve their writing and learn to write particular things—including those on the mandated writing tests. (For lots more ideas about helping children learn to write fluently, see *Classrooms That Work,* Cunningham & Allington, 2003.)

Rereading Develops Fluency

One of the major ways that we become fluent readers is to read something over several times. At first, a lot of our attention is on identifying the words. The second time we are able to read in phrases as our brain puts the phrases together into meaningful units. The third time we read more rapidly with good expression and in a seemingly "effortless" way. There are various ways to include repeated readings as part of your classroom routines. In this section, we will describe five ways many teachers have found to work well with children across the elementary grades: echo reading, choral reading, timed repeated reading, paired repeated reading, and taped reading/listening.

Echo Reading

One teacher had been doing echo reading for months when a child suddenly asked, "What's an echo?" The teacher tried to explain it and discovered that many children hadn't heard an echo. After some "field research," the teacher located a spot in the auditorium where sound would echo, and the class all got to hear their voices echoing back to them. Echo reading made a lot more sense to them after that and they tried to "be the echo." It is easy to forget that our children don't know everything we know. If your children haven't heard an echo, you might try to find a place to take them where they can have firsthand experience with echoes.

Echo reading is usually done one sentence at a time. We often do echo reading with short, easy text that has only one sentence on a page. Echo reading is fun to do when the text has different voices. *Brown Bear, Brown Bear* (Bill Martin, Jr., 1970), *I Went Walking* (Sue Williams, 1990), and *Hattie and the Fox* (Mem Fox, 1988) are favorites for echo reading. Echo reading also works well for stories such as *There's an Alligator Under My Bed* in which one boy is telling the story. Stories told in the first-person format are called "I" stories. When we echo-read "I" stories, we try to sound the way the different voices would sound. Some favorite "I" stories include *One of Three* by Angela Johnson (1991), *Enzo the Wonderfish* by Cathy Wilcox (1993), and *My Friend* by Taro Gomi (1990).

Echo reading is also appropriate for reading plays. We read the whole play in an echo-reading format first, using different voices for the different characters. As we read, we ask children to think about each character and which character they would like to be and then read the play again.

Children love plays and teachers tell us they would use more plays if they had multiple copies of easy plays. This is one of the few good uses of copying machines. You can easily take a favorite story and turn it into a play script. All of the fairy tales make good and easy plays. Children love reading and playing *The Little Red Hen, The Gingerbread Man, The Three Pigs,* and *The Three Billy Goats Gruff.* The nice thing about writing out and copying simple scripts for these classic stories is that you can let the children take them home. Make their homework assignment to gather as many actors as they can and read the play at home. Parents love helping with this kind of homework and say they wish they had had homework like that when they were in school.

Choral Reading

Choral reading works best for poetry, refrains, and books with lots of conversation. The whole class can read or you can assign groups and parts. Teachers use old favorites including nursery rhymes and finger plays. *Itsy Bitsy Spider, Five Little Pumpkins, Rudolph the Red-Nosed Reindeer,* and *Peter Cottontail* are naturals for choral reading. Choral reading is a wonderful way to reread books such as *The Lion and the Mouse* and *Brown Bear, Brown Bear* in which characters talk to each other. Choral reading should be used throughout the grades because rereading provides children with the practice needed to build fluency and self-confidence.

Nursery rhymes and other rhymes and finger plays are naturals for choral reading. Begin by reading the rhyme to the children. You may want to echo-read it with them a time or two. If you have the rhyme in a Big Book, use that. If not, reproduce it on a chart. After reading it together, children enjoy pantomiming these rhymes while other children read them.

Taped Reading/Listening

Another way teachers provide opportunities for children to do repeated readings is to provide children with opportunities to read along with an audiotape of a book or story. There are lots of variations on this activity and lots of different names for it. Be patient and allow the student to listen to or read the selection during any free time or at home. When the student is able to read the selection fluently without the aid of the tape, he or she should receive praise and ample opportunities to read the selection to parents, other teachers, fellow students, and young children in kindergarten or first grade. Although the student has not really memorized the selection (the student could not read the selection without having the book to follow), a combination of memorization and reading enables the student to have the real experience of successful, effective, and fluent reading. Several students can receive such instruction simultaneously, each one with a different book. The limit is defined by how many tape recorders are available. Or a group of students can learn the same book simultaneously if you have multiple copies of an appropriate book or magazine articles. Find a selection that would interest the student and that is not too long or too difficult. Choose a selection that is appealing and can be read dramatically. Then instruct the student to listen to the tape and follow along in the book until he or she can read it fluently.

Timed Repeated Reading

For timed repeated reading, you need a passage of interest to the student that is at the student's instructional level. The passage should be short, no more than 150 words. Give the student the passage and tell him or her to read it silently and to get ready to read it orally with few errors and at a comfortable rate. After silent reading, have the student read the passage to you, count the oral reading errors (the three most frequently occurring errors are words left out, words changed, and words added in), and time the reading. If the student makes more than five errors per hundred words, the passage is too difficult to use, and an easier one should be chosen. If no more than five errors per hundred words are made by the student, tell the reader the time it took and help her or him correct any errors. Then have the student practice reading the material again. Repeat this process until the student has read the passage three or four times. While some students are practicing, another can be reading to you, which makes it possible to use repeated readings with a small group of readers.

Paired Repeated Reading

Paired repeated reading is just like repeated reading but without timing. In other words, the student reads and rereads a passage to make fewer errors, not to increase rate. Students can be paired for perfection or repeated reading. They like listening to each other read to count errors. Teachers should make sure, however, that students do not interrupt each other during reading but wait until the selection is finished before helping the reader make corrections.

Fluency Development Lessons

In 1998, Tim Rasinski and Nancy Padak published a study that drew everyone's attention to how widespread fluency problems are for disabled readers. They had looked at a large number of remedial readers and evaluated their abilities in three areas: comprehension, decoding, and fluency. Almost all the children were well below grade level in all three areas, but fluency was by far the biggest area of concern. The children read the test passages in such a slow and laborious manner that the investigators were surprised that they had any comprehension at all. In response to their findings, Rasinski and Padak developed a lesson for teaching fluency they call a fluency development lesson, or FDL (Rasinski & Padak, 2001). Here is how the fluency development lesson strategy works. This is adapted from a more detailed and rich explanation in Tim Rasinski's (2003) wonderfully practical book, *The Fluent Reader.*

The teacher chooses a short passage—often a poem—that is apt to be appealing to the children and reads the passage aloud to the children several times, modeling fluent reading. Meaning for the poem or passage and for any difficult vocabulary words is built through discussion with the children.

Using individual copies of the poem or with the poem written on a chart, the teacher and the class do a choral reading of the poem. The poem is read chorally several times, often with different children reading different parts or verses.

The children are paired and take turns reading the passage to each other. Each person reads the passage three times. The children help each other and respond to each other's reading with praise, support, and encouragement.

When the class gathers together again, children can volunteer to read the passage aloud for everyone. In some cases, children might read the passage to other classes or to other school personnel.

Each child chooses two or three words from the passage to add to their personal word banks. They study these words and often use them in a variety of word sorts and games.

Children put one copy of the text in their poetry folder. They are given a second copy to take home. Children are encouraged to read the passage to whoever will listen. Children and parents alike report that this is one "homework" assignment they all look forward to.

The following day, the previous day's passage is read again and then the whole cycle begins with a new passage. Rasinski suggests a fast pace for this activity and estimates that once the class learns the routines, the whole FDL can be completed in 15–20 minutes.

Fluency development lessons are easy to do and are enjoyed by both teachers and students. Rasinski reports that children engaged in these lessons made greater gains in reading than a similar group of children who read the same passages but did not use the FDL procedure. Fluency development lessons would be a welcome addition to any classroom routine but would be especially helpful in remedial and special education classes.

 Summary

Developing fluency needs to be one of the major goals of reading instruction. When children are first starting to read, their reading is not apt to be fluent. They must stop at almost all the words and take a second or two to recognize the word or figure it out. Fluency develops when children do lots of reading and writing—including lots of easy text. Repeated reading helps children develop fluency because with each reading their word identification becomes quicker and more automatic, freeing attention for expression, phrasing, and comprehension. Fluency development lessons are enjoyable and help all children become fluent readers. They are especially important for children whose reading is well below grade level.

In English, words such as *of, said, the, have, they,* and many others occur in almost every text we read. These words are called high-frequency words because they occur so frequently in everything we read and write. In order to read and write fluently, children need to instantly recognize and spell these high-frequency words. Building this automatic and rapid recognition and spelling of high-frequency words is the topic of the next chapter.

chapter 6

High-Frequency Words

One hundred words account for almost half of all the words we read and write (Fry, Fountoukidis, & Polk, 1985). Ten words—*the, of, and, a, to, in, is, you, that,* and *it*—account for almost one-quarter of all the words we read and write. As soon as possible, children should learn to read and spell these high-frequency words.

When children at an early age learn to recognize and automatically spell the most frequently occurring words, all their attention is freed for decoding and spelling less frequent words and, more important, for processing meaning. Stopping to figure out a new word while reading, or stopping to say the word slowly and figure out how you might spell it while writing, requires time and mental energy. In fact, stopping to think about a new word takes your attention away from meaning. Psychologists explain that we all have limited attention spans, sometimes called short-term memory. Short-term memory is the place that holds words or other bits of information. The short-term memory span for most people is about seven words. When we read, we hold the words in short-term memory until we have enough words to make meaning from them. Meaning can then go into long-term memory. Thus, we make meaning from the words stored in short-term memory and send that meaning to long-term memory. This frees up all our short-term memory space for more words, and the process continues. So it goes, until we need our short-term memory space for something else—like figuring out the pronunciation of a new word. Writing works the same way. We spell most words automatically, and when we have to stop to figure out the spelling of a word, our attention moves from what we are writing to how to spell a particular word.

Decoding or figuring out the spelling of a new word takes all our short-term memory space. In fact, when this decoding process begins, all words already read or written and stored in short-term memory are dumped out (into the garbage disposal, I think). This dumping explains why, once the new word is decoded or spelled, we must quickly reread any prior words in that sentence so that we may put them in short-term memory again. It also explains why children who have to decode many words often don't know what they have read after they read it! Their short-term memory space keeps getting preempted for decoding tasks, and they can't reread every sentence over and over. So they never get enough words in short-term memory from which to make meaning to put in long-term memory. All their attention is required for figuring out words, and there is no capacity for putting together meaning. In order to read and write fluently with comprehension and meaning, children must be able to automatically read and spell the most frequent words. As the store of words they can automatically read and spell increases, so will their speed and comprehension.

The second reason we want children to automatically recognize and spell high-frequency words is that many of the most frequent words are not pronounced or spelled in logical ways: If *the* were pronounced like other words with the same spelling pattern, it would rhyme with *he, me,* and *be; to* would rhyme with *go, no,* and *so; said* would rhyme with *maid* and *paid;* and *have* would rhyme with *cave* and *wave.* If *they, was,* and *come* were spelled logically, they would be spelled the way many children spell them—t-h-a-y, w-u-z, c-u-m.

The apparent lack of logic in how the most frequent words are spelled and pronounced has a logical—and historical—explanation. The way we pronounce words changes with use. The words used most often are, of course, the words whose pronunciation has changed the most. In most cases, pronunciation shifts to an easier pronunciation. It is quicker and easier to get your tongue in position to say "the" in the usual way than it is to make it rhyme with *he, me,* and *we.* "Said" takes longer to say if you make it rhyme with *paid* and *maid.* Children should learn to read and spell the most frequently occurring words because these are the words they will read and write over and over. Many of them cannot be decoded, and if you spell them logically, you will often be wrong.

The problem is that many struggling readers have a great deal of difficulty learning these words. They often know them today and forget them tomorrow. This chapter will focus on strategies that have been successful in teaching everyone—even the children who need multiple practices—to read and spell the most frequent words.

Building Meaning for High-Frequency Words

The first problem many children have with the high-frequency words is that most of these have no meaning. Unlike *dinosaur, apples,* and *happy,* words like *are, is,* and *have* are functional, connecting, abstract words children cannot connect any meaning to. How do you explain, demonstrate, or otherwise make sense of words like *of, for,* and *from?* In addition, what meaning they do have changes from minute to minute. *There* is the opposite of *here,* but if you move across the room, there becomes here! *This* becomes *that* and *these* become *those.*

In addition to the problems these words create by having no concrete consistent meaning, many of the frequently occurring words share the same letters. Besides the often confused *of, for,* and *from* and the reversible words *on/no, was/saw,* beginners are always confusing the *th* and the *w* words:

the	there	their	this	that
they	them	then	these	those

what	want	went	when	who
why	were	where	will	with

To many children, remembering these words is like trying to remember the pronunciation of words in a foreign language when you don't know what they mean and they don't follow any standard spelling system. No wonder they know them today and forget them tomorrow.

What kind of activities can we provide to ensure that all children will learn to read and write these critical words? The most important factor to consider in teaching the highly frequent words seems to be the meaning—or, more specifically, the lack of meaning—factor.

In Chapter Four, we discussed learning letter names and how children who knew some concrete words that contained the letters remembered the letters better because they had associated the letters with the already-known words. Associative learning is always more permanent than rote learning. Since these frequent words have no meaning in and of themselves, we must help the children associate them with something meaningful. To introduce the word *of,* for example, we might have pictures of a piece of pie, a can of Coke, and a box of cookies. These pictures would be labeled *a piece of pie, a can of Coke, a box of cookies* with the word *of* underlined. Next, the children would think of other things they like to eat and drink with the word *of,* such as a glass of milk, a bowl of soup, a piece of bubble gum. The labeled pictures would then be displayed to help students associate meaning with this abstract word as in Figure 6.1.

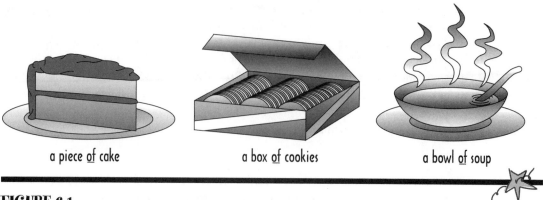

a piece <u>of</u> cake   a box <u>of</u> cookies   a bowl <u>of</u> soup

FIGURE 6.1
Picture Posters to Build Meaning for the Word *of*

After an abstract word is associated with meaning, there must be practice with that word. This practice can take many forms, but it should not consist solely of looking at the word and saying it. Not all children are good visual learners. Many children need to do something in order to learn something. Chanting the spelling of words and writing the words provide children with auditory and kinesthetic routes to learning and remembering abstract words.

Once the children can associate meaning with a word such as *of* and have practiced *of* enough times to be able to read it and spell it, it is time to introduce one of the words with which *of* is often confused, such as *for.* You might simply extend the picture posters already made for *of* by attaching another piece of paper to each and writing the word *for* and the name of one of the children in your class. Underline the *for* and your posters now look like Figure 6.2.

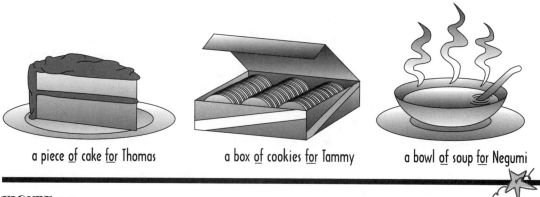

a piece <u>of</u> cake <u>for</u> Thomas   a box <u>of</u> cookies <u>for</u> Tammy   a bowl <u>of</u> soup <u>for</u> Negumi

FIGURE 6.2
Picture Posters to Build Meaning for the Words *of* and *for*

Have children name foods and tell who they are for; then provide chanting and writing practice with both the words *for* and *of.*

When *of* and *for* are firmly associated and can be read and written, teach *from.* For each difficult word, think of some picture or sentence association your children would understand. Perhaps you have some children who came to your school from other states or countries. You could make some sentence posters with sentences such as:

Billy is *from* California.
José is *from* Mexico.

The children can then associate meaning with the word *from* because they know where these two classmates come from. Then provide practice with *of, for,* and *from.*

How much meaning you have to build for words and how much practice will be required to learn them varies with the different words and for different children. In general, the more abstract a word is and the more similar-looking abstract words there are, the more association and practice will be required to learn them. The following are the three principles for teaching the frequently occurring word:

1. Provide a way for students to associate meaning with the words.
2. Once meaning is associated, provide practice using a variety of learning modes.
3. If a common word has many easily confused words, teach one first. As soon as that one is learned, teach another and practice both. Then teach a third and practice all three.

Doing a Word Wall

Children need to associate meaning with the abstract connecting words, and they need to have them displayed in some readily accessible place so that they can find them when they need them while reading and writing. Many teachers display these words on the wall or on a bulletin board. They "have" a word wall. For struggling readers, having a word wall is not sufficient. You have to "do" the word wall.

Doing the word wall is not the same thing as having a word wall. Having a word wall might mean putting all these words up somewhere in the room and telling students to use them. Most struggling readers can't use them because they don't know them and don't know which is which! Doing a word wall means:

1. being selective and limiting the words to those really common words that children need a lot in writing
2. adding words gradually—five a week

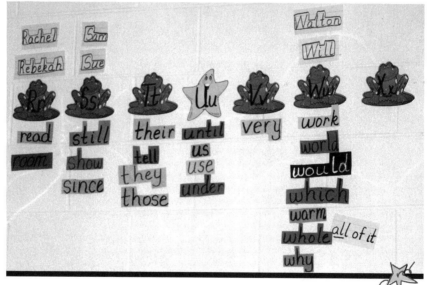

These word walls are used to make frequently used words accessible to students.

3. making words accessible by putting them where everyone can see them, writing them in big black letters, and using a variety of colors so that the constantly confused words (*for, from, that, them, they, this,* etc.) have different colors

4. practicing the words by chanting and writing them, because struggling readers are not usually good visual learners and can't just look at and remember words

5. doing a variety of review activities to provide enough practice so that the words are read and spelled instantly and automatically

6. making sure that word-wall words are spelled correctly in any writing students do

Teachers who "do" word walls (rather than just have word walls) report that *all* their children can learn these critical words.

Selecting Words for the Wall

The selection of the words varies from classroom to classroom, but the selection principle is the same. We include words students will need often in their reading and writing and that are often confused with other words. First-grade teachers who are using a reading series usually select some highly frequent words taught in those books. Other teachers select their words from a high-frequency word list. In addition to high-frequency words, first-grade teachers often begin their word walls with the names of their children and add an example word for each letter in the alphabet—even if there is no high-frequency word for that letter.

Beyond first grade, we look for words commonly misspelled in the children's writing and add them to the wall. Children frequently misspell homophones, and these can be added with a picture or phrase clue attached to all but one of the words. For example, we add a card with the number 2 next to *two* and attach the word *also* and the phrase *too late* next to *too*. Children learn to think about whether they are writing the number *two*, the "too late *too*," or "the other one." Once high-frequency words are on the wall, teachers may add words with a particular pattern—beginning letters, rhyming pattern, vowel pattern, ending—to provide an example for this pattern.

Displaying the Words

The words are written with a thick, black-ink, permanent marker on pieces of different colored paper. Words are placed on the wall above or below the letter they begin with. When easily confused words are added, we make sure they are on a different color paper from the other words they are usually confused with. Cutting around the configuration is another helpful cue to those easily confused words. Children who are looking for *where* tend to distinguish it from *were* by its "*h* sticking up." Most teachers add five new words each week and do at least one daily activity in which the children find, chant, and write the words.

Chanting and Writing the Words

To begin the word-wall practice, students number a sheet of paper from one to five. The teacher calls out five words, putting each word in a sentence. As the teacher calls out each

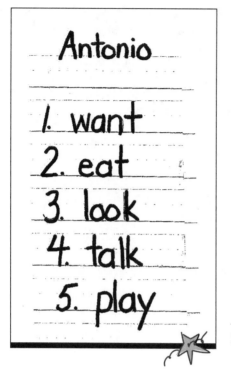

FIGURE 6.3
Word-Wall Words Written

word, a child finds and points to that word on the wall. Next, the students clap and chant the spelling of each word in a rhythmic fashion. After chanting, they write each word. Many teachers tie this daily writing of five words into handwriting instruction and model for the children how to make each letter as the children write the words. When all five words have been written, the teacher leads the students to check or fix their own papers. On the day new words are added, the new words are called out, clapped, chanted, and written. These new words are often reviewed on the second day. During the rest of the week, however, any five words from the wall can be called out. Words with which children need much practice are called out almost every day. (See Figure 6.3.)

 "On-the-Back" Activities

Most teachers allot 10 minutes each day for the daily word-wall practice. Early in the year, it takes the whole 10 minutes to call out, chant, write, and check five words. As the year goes on, children become much faster at chanting, writing, and checking the words and can do five words in 5–6 minutes. At this point, we add an "on-the-back" activity (called this because we have them turn over their word-wall paper and do this

High-Utility Wall Words

Teachers make their own decisions about which words to add to their word walls by observing which words children use frequently in their writing. This list is intended to be an example of the kinds of words that might be included if the word wall is to have the highest utility for the children. This list has high utility in multiple ways:

It includes the most frequent words—those that make up 50 percent of the words children read and write.

There is an example word for each initial consonant: *b, c, d, f, g, h, j, k, l, m, n, p, r, s, t, v, w, y, z* (including both common sounds for *c* and *g*).

There is an example for the most common blends: *bl, br, cl, cr, dr, fl, fr, gr, pl, pr, sk, sl, sm, sn, sp, st, str,* and *tr;* the common digraphs *ch, sh, th, wh;* and the two-letter combinations *ph, wr, kn, qu.*

There is an example for the most common vowel spelling patterns:

at	make	rain	day	car	saw	caught
went	eat	see	her	new		
in	like	night	girl	thing		
not	those	coat	go	for	how	slow	out	boy	look	school
us	use	hurt				
my	very					

There is an example for the highest-utility phonograms (Wylie & Durrell, 1970):

ack	ail	ain	ake	ale	ame	an	ank	ap	ash
at	ate	aw	ay	eat	ell	est	ice	ick	ide
ight	ill	in	ine	ing	ink	ip	it	ock	oke
op	ore	ot	uck	ug	ump	unk			

It includes the most common contractions: *can't, didn't, don't, it's, won't,* and the most common homophones: *to, too, two; their, they're, there; right, write; no, know; one, won.*

It includes words such as *favorite, teacher, school, family,* and *sister,* which young children use frequently in their writing.

Ideally, a classroom word wall would add five words per week and have about 100–120 words by the end of the year. This list contains 180 words, which is too many for any one word wall. In some schools, first-grade teachers pick the most frequent words for their walls. Second-grade teachers begin the year by gradually putting up some of the first-grade words that are particularly hard to spell—*they, were, because,* and so forth—and then add others.

about	don't	it	phone	they're
after	down	it's	play	thing
all	drink	joke	presents	this
am	each	jump	pretty	those
an	eat	junk	question	time
and	family	kick	rain	to
animal	father	know	ride	too
are	favorite	like	right	trip
as	first	line	run	truck
at	fly	little	said	two
be	for	long	sale	up
because	friend	look	saw	us
been	from	made	school	use
best	fun	mail	see	very
big	get	make	she	want
black	girl	many	sister	was
boy	give	me	slow	way
brother	go	more	skate	we
bug	good	mother	small	went
but	green	my	snap	were
by	gym	name	so	what
call	had	new	some	when
can	has	nice	sports	where
can't	have	night	stop	which
car	he	no	street	who
caught	her	not	talk	why
children	here	now	teacher	will
city	him	of	tell	with
clock	his	off	than	won
coat	house	old	thank	won't
come	how	on	that	would
could	hurt	one	the	write
crash	I	or	their	you
day	if	other	them	your
did	in	out	then	zoo
didn't	into	over	there	
do	is	people	they	

activity on the back). The on-the-back activity is designed to provide additional practice with word-wall words or to help children learn that some of the words on the wall can help them spell lots of other words. Several of the most popular and productive on-the-back activities are described next.

Easy Rhyming Activity

Half the high-frequency words do not follow the logical patterns—but half do. Many teachers put a star or sticker on word-wall words that children can use to help them spell lots of rhyming words. This activity helps children learn how to use the starred words to spell lots of other words. To begin this activity, the teacher might say something like:

> "All of the words we have on our word wall are important words because we see them over and over again in the books we read and they help us write. But some words are important in another way. Some of the words on our wall will help us spell lots of other words that rhyme with them. *It* is one of those helpful words."

The teacher circles *it*, which was one of the five words called out today.

> "Today, we are going to practice using *it* to spell five other words we use a lot in our writing. Turn your paper over and number from one to five. The first word *it* will help you spell is *bit*. You might be writing about how your brother got **bit** by a dog. Let's say *bit* slowly and listen for the first sound. Yes, *bit* begins with the letter *b*. Everyone write *b*. Now, words that rhyme usually have the same spelling pattern. The spelling pattern in a short word begins with the vowel and continues until the end of the word. Because *it* begins with a vowel, *i*, the whole word *it* is also the spelling pattern. Write *i-t* after *b* and you can spell *bit*."

The on-the-back lesson continues as the teacher gives them possible scenarios in which they would need to use *it* to help them spell a rhyming word:

> "What if you were writing about the baseball game and wanted to say you got a **hit?** Say *hit* slowly. Write the first letter, *h*, and then finish the rhyming word with the spelling pattern *i-t*."
>
> "You might be writing about how you taught your dog to **sit**." Everyone writes *s-i-t*.

"You might write about going to the mall to buy a new winter jacket be-cause last year's jacket wouldn't **fit.**"

"The last rhyming word is one that begins with two letters. What if you're writing about your cat and want to tell that when she is really mad, she will **spit** at something? Say *spit* slowly with me, stretching it out and listening for two sounds at the beginning. Good, you hear an *s* and a *p*. Now finish your word with the *i-t* pattern."

For the on-the-back rhyming activity, we have children write five words that we choose that rhyme with one of the word-wall words, as shown in Figure 6.4. We put it in a "What if you are writing and need to spell" context because knowing how rhyming words help you spell other words is only useful if you do it when you are writing and trying to spell a word. We use several examples, trying to choose words they might actually need to write. In most lessons, we include some words with sin-gle beginning letters and others where you have to listen for two letters. We model how you "stretch out the word," listening for the beginning sound, and then finish the word with the spelling pattern—the vowel and what follows.

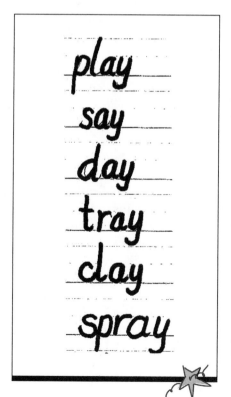

FIGURE 6.4
Rhyming Words for the Word *play* Written on the Back of the Word-Wall Paper

If you have the word *eat* on your word wall, you might have students spell rhyming words by having them pretend they are writing sentences such as:

I hope Wake will **beat** Carolina this Saturday.
We had a storm, and the **heat** was off at my house.
We had company, and I had to get my room clean and **neat.**
I was good at school, so my Dad took me to the mall for a **treat.**
Some kids will try to **cheat** to win the game.

When you do these rhyming activities, be sure to give them the rhyming word rather than ask them to tell you rhyming words. Some rhymes have more than one pattern, and by controlling which words you have them spell, you can avoid using words such as *feet* and *Pete,* which have another pattern. They will eventually have to learn to use their visual checking system to determine the correct pattern, but the first step is to get them spelling by pattern rather than putting down one letter for each sound. Here are a few more examples for starred words from the word wall.

At will help you spell *cat, bat, hat, brat,* and *flat.*
Look will help you spell *cook, book, hook, brook,* and *crook.*
Went will help you spell *bent, dent, tent, sent,* and *spent.*
Not will help you spell *hot, got, lot, spot,* and *trot.*
Am will help you spell *ham, Sam, Pam, clam,* and *Spam.*
And will help you spell *hand, sand, band, stand,* and *brand.*
Can will help you spell *Dan, man, ran, tan,* and *plan.*
Will will help you spell *Bill, fill, pill, still,* and *spill.*
Make will help you spell *bake, cake, rake, lake,* and *shake.*

Harder Rhyming Activity

There is another rhyming "on-the-back" format that is harder but closer to what children actually have to do to use the word-wall words to spell a word they need while writing. To do this rhyming format, make sure that all the words you call out for them to write on the front have some words that rhyme and share the same spelling pattern. You might call out the words *make, thing, like, went,* and *will.* Help the children to notice that all these words are helpful words (starred or stickered words if they are so on your wall). Tell them that you are going to pretend to be writing and need to spell a word that rhymes with one of these five words. Tell them some sentences you might be writing, emphasizing the word you need to spell, and let them decide which of the five helpful words they wrote on the front will help you.

We like to cook chicken on the *grill.*
I was so scared I started to *shake* all over.

My brother *spent* his whole allowance on baseball cards.
We are going to *sing* at my church on Sunday morning.
I want a new *bike* for my birthday.

Once you have begun to use this new rhyming format, alternate it with the easier one in which your sentences use rhymes for only one of the words. The harder one helps children who are ready to learn how thinking of a rhyming word can help them spell lots of words. The easier format is still important for children who are still developing their sense of rhyme and how rhyme helps us spell.

Easy Ending Activity

Another on-the-back activity helps children learn how to spell word-wall words that need an ending. Imagine that the five word-wall words you called out for them to locate, cheer for, and write were:

girl   boy   friend   brother   sister

Have them turn their papers over and write the words *boys, sisters, brothers, friends,* and *girls.*

On another day, call out five words that can have *ed* endings, such as *want, look, jump, kick,* and *play.* Then have them write these words with the *ed* ending on the back. On another day, do a similar activity with words to which *ing* can be added.

For the easy endings activities, we limit the ending to just one, and we don't include words that need spelling changes. Once students get good at adding *s, ed,* and *ing,* we do some more complex on-the-back activities with endings.

Harder Ending Activity

Make your on-the-back activity with endings more complex by including different words and endings. Imagine that your students have written these five words on the front of their paper:

want   eat   look   talk   play

Have them turn their papers over. Then say something like:

"Today we are going to work on how to spell these word-wall words when they need a different ending. I will say some sentences that some of you might write, and you listen for the word-wall word that has had an ending added:

My friends and I love *eating* at McDonald's.
We were *looking* for some new shoes.

I was *talking* on the phone to my Grandma.

My mom *wants* the new baby to be a girl.

My friend spent the night and we *played* Nintendo till 11:00."

After each sentence, the children identify the word-wall word and the ending, decide how to spell it, and write it on their papers.

As the children get good at adding *s, ed,* and *ing,* include some endings with spelling changes—the *e* dropped, a *y* changed to *i,* or a letter doubled. Since the teacher and children decide ahead of time what to write, everyone is writing them correctly, and this additional information about how to spell words with a variety of endings and spelling changes really moves the accelerated learners along in their writing ability. (See Figure 6.5.)

When students are good at spelling word-wall words with the most common endings, include some words in which *y, ly, er,* and *est* are added. Show them how they can spell *jumpy, rainy,* and *funny* by adding *y* to *jump, rain,* and *fun,* and how to spell *nicely* and *friendly* by adding *ly.* You can add *er* and *est* to *new, little,* and *pretty. Talk, jump, kick, ride, make, eat,* and *quit* can become the person who does them by adding *er.* Of course, you will help them decide what spelling changes they need as they write these words.

Combining Rhyme and Endings

Once your children are good at spelling words that rhyme with word-wall words and adding endings, it is time to combine these two formats. Begin with an easy rhyming

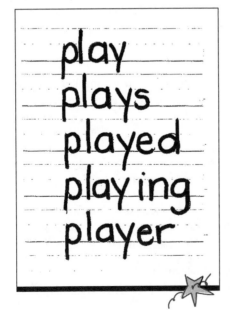

FIGURE 6.5
An On-the-Back Activity with Endings Added to *play*

format in which the words rhyme with just one word-wall word and have endings added. Here is an example using the word-wall word *down*. The sentences the teacher says in which the children need to identify a word with an ending that rhymes with **down** might be:

> My favorite thing at the circus was the **clowns.**
> I saw the teacher **frowning** at me.
> In the play, I was **crowned** the king.
> My little brother fell in the pool and almost **drowned.**
> I have lived in three different **towns.**

You could also do this with the harder format. When children are writing, they often need to spell a word that rhymes with one of the word-wall words and has an ending added. Make sure, however, that everyone spells the word aloud correctly before writing it, because this could be frustrating for many of your children. The children have written the words *tell, school, but, make,* and *rain* on the front.

> My sister won the third-grade **spelling** bee.
> I am going swimming as soon as the **pools** open.
> My brother makes money **cutting** all the lawns in the neighborhood.
> We almost had a wreck when the **brakes** didn't work on our truck.
> I **trained** my dog to stay when I tell him to.

Be a Mind Reader

Be a Mind Reader is a favorite on-the-back activity. In this game, the teacher thinks of a word on the wall and then gives five clues to that word. Choose a word and write it on a scrap of paper, but do not let the students see what word you have written. Have students number their paper one to five, and tell them that you are going to see who can read your mind and figure out which of the words on the board you are thinking of and have written on your paper. Tell them you will give them five clues. By the fifth clue, everyone should guess your word, but if they read your mind they might get it before the fifth clue. For your first clue, always give the same clue: "It's one of the words on the wall." Students should write next to number one the word they think it might be. Each succeeding clue should narrow down what it can be until by clue five there is only one possible word. As you give clues, students write the word they believe it is next to each number. If succeeding clues confirm the word a student has written next to one number, the student writes that word again by the next number. Clues may include any features of the word you want students to notice. (It has more than two letters. It has less than four letters. It has an *e*. It does not have a *t.*) After clue five, show students the word you wrote on your scratch paper and say, "I know you all have the word next to number five, but who has it next to number four? Three? Two?

One?" Some students will have read your mind and will be pleased as punch with themselves! Here are clues for the word *them*.

1. It's one of the words on the wall.
2. It has four letters.
3. It begins with *th*.
4. The vowel is an *e*.
5. It finishes the sentence *I gave my books to* _____.

Ruler Tap

A ruler is used for another activity. The teacher calls out a word and then taps out several letters in that word without saying those letters. When the tapping stops, the teacher calls on a child to finish spelling the word out loud. If the child correctly finishes spelling the word, that child gets to call out a word and tap some of the letters. Everyone writes each word after each word is tapped and spelled.

Other Word-Wall Practice Activities

In addition to the on-the-back activities that take just a few minutes of time after students write five words on the front, there are two popular activities that take a little longer but help students practice these critical high-frequency words. The children see both WORDO and the word sorts as games and often ask to play them during indoor recess.

WORDO

WORDO is a variation of the ever-popular Bingo game. Children love it and don't know they are getting a lot of practice reading and writing highly frequent words. All you need to play WORDO are some photocopied sheets on which 9 or 25 blocks have been drawn in (see Figure 6.6) and some small pieces of paper or objects for students to use to cover words as they fill in the blocks. Reproduce a good supply of these grid sheets and you are ready when the assembly program is canceled or the foreign language teacher suddenly quits.

Call on students to pick words from the wall they want included in the game. As each word is picked, students will write it on their WORDO sheets in a blank block they choose, and you will write it on an index card. (Make sure students understand that, unlike its Bingo counterpart, in WORDO all children will ultimately have all the same words that are called out. Since they will have written them in different places, however, there will still be winners. Unfortunately, you can't play for a full card.)

FIGURE 6.6
Blank WORDO Sheets

When all students have filled up their sheets with the 9 or 25 words called out, you are ready to play. Shuffle your index cards and call the words one at a time. Have students chant the spelling of each word and then cover it with paper squares or small objects. The first student to have a complete row covered wins WORDO. Be sure to have the winner tell you the words covered and check to see that the words have been called. Students can then clear their sheets and play again. You might let the winner become the next caller and you can play the winner's sheet. Children love watching their teachers lose.

Word Sorts

Word sorts can be done with the words on the wall or any group of words the teacher wants students to concentrate on. The purpose of word sorts is to focus student attention on the various features of the words. To do a word sort, write 10–15 words on large index cards and have students write these words on separate slips of paper. Have the students sort the words into different piles, depending on some features certain words share. Students may sort all words with a certain number of letters, all words that begin with a certain letter, or all words that have a certain letter anywhere in them.

Sometimes the teacher tells the students the criterion on which to sort, for example, all words with an *a* in them. Other times, the teacher tells students which words to select—*boy, try, my, day*—and the students must guess how these words are all alike. In this case, these are all words that end in the letter *y*. Sorting words based on the number of letters and on the different letters and sounds represented by the letters helps students attend to those letters.

Words can also be sorted according to semantic features. Students might choose all the things or all the words that name people. Words that describe things, words that tell what you can do, and words that name things found outside are just some of the many possibilities for sorting based on semantic features. Once students understand the various ways the words can be sorted, they can play the role of teacher and tell which words to choose or a criterion for sorting the words.

Portable and Take-Home Word Walls

Portable word walls such as those in Figure 6.7 were invented by an enterprising re-medial-reading teacher whose third graders complained that they couldn't "write good" in her room because they didn't have their word wall. Upon investigation, it was

A	B	C		D	E	F
are	before	can't		don't	enough	first
also		could				favorite
about						

G	H	I		J	K	L
getting	have	I'm			know	let's
		into			knew	

M	N	O		P	Q	R
myself	new	one		people		really
		our				

S	T	U	V	W	X	YZ
said	then	until	very	want		your
school	there			was		you're
	threw			wear		
	to			whether		

FIGURE 6.7
A Portable Word Wall Made from a File Folder

discovered that their classroom teacher had a colorful word wall and that these re-medial readers used the wall to spell highly frequent words as they wrote. Any thought of constructing a word wall in the remedial teacher's room was quickly dismissed when the teacher remembered her room was really a closet and that other teachers used this space. The problem was solved by constructing portable word walls made of file folders divided alphabetically. The classroom teacher, the remedial teacher, and the students worked together to copy all the words on the wall to the folders, using per-manent markers the same color as the paper on which wall words were written. Then, each week, as five words were added to the classroom word wall, the teacher and students added them to their portable word walls. The students took their word walls to remedial reading and home for the summer. Perhaps they even took them to fourth grade the next year.

Take-home word walls are also used by some teachers in addition to the word walls in the classroom. Some teachers reproduce a sheet and send it home each week or month with the new words added. Students are told to have their take home word wall out as they do homework because word-wall words must be spelled correctly in everything they write.

 ## Theme Boards

Word-wall space is reserved for really important words—words we want all students to learn to read and spell automatically, fluently, correctly, every time, everywhere! In every classroom there are other words students need—but the need changes as units, topics, and themes change. In addition to a word wall, most elementary classrooms have a theme board on which to display these words. The words on the board change as units, topics, and themes change.

❧ March Words ❧		
wind	sunny	Easter
storm	good luck	vacation
kite	flowers	rabbit
tornado	daffodils	bunny
severe weather	crocus	hop hun
lion	Japan	rainbow
lamb	leprechaun	beach
St. Patrick's Day	bloom	short sleeve
clovers	green grass	dying eggs

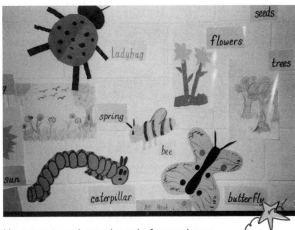

Here are two theme boards from primary classrooms.

Summary: How Fluency Activities and Word Walls Are Multilevel

Two of the major activities for developing fluency—independent reading and daily writing—are automatically multilevel. When children read independently something of their own choosing, they are reading on their level. When you write, you can only write on your level. Repeated Reading and Fluency Development lessons can be made multilevel if the teacher selects text for different children to read that is appropriate to their level.

If you watched children doing the daily word-wall practice, you might assume that they are all learning the same thing—how to spell words. But what they are doing externally may not reveal what they are processing internally. Imagine that the five new words added to the wall one week were *come, where, they, boy,* and *friend.* During the daily word-wall practice, the children who have already learned to read them are learning to spell them. Other children, however, who require lots of practice with words, are learning to read them. Once each child has practiced them enough to be able to read them (and the number varies from child to child and word to word), the same daily word-wall practice will help them learn to spell the words.

On-the-back activities that extend word-wall words to the spelling of rhyming words and words with endings provide something to be learned for your accelerated students. Teachers who do these activities regularly report that the best readers in the class not only spell all the word-wall words correctly but also spell uncommon rhyming words and words with endings. If you practice handwriting each day as you write the word-wall words, all children get some handwriting instruction—often needed by both struggling and advanced readers.

Using Phonics and Spelling Patterns

Most of the words we read and write are one and two-syllable *regular* words, which, because they are consistent with the rules of spelling and pronunciation, we can decode and spell even if we have not seen them before. Developing the ability to independently read and write most regular words is a complex process and takes time and practice with a variety of activities.

In English, the vowels are variant and unpredictable. The letter *a* commonly represents the sound in *and, made, agree, art, talk,* and *care.* We have given names to some of these sounds. *And* has a short *a; made* has a long *a; agree* is a schwa; the *a* in *art* is *r* controlled. We don't even have names for the sound *a* represents in *talk* and *care.* Further complicating things are the many words in which *a* doesn't do any of these six common things—*eat, coat, legal*—and the fact that even the consistent sounds can be spelled in many different ways. The long *a* sound is commonly spelled by the patterns in *made, maid,* and *may.* The sound *a* has in *talk* is spelled by an *aw* in *saw* and an *au* in *Paul.*

When you stop to think about all the possible sounds and spelling patterns for the vowels, you marvel at the fact that anyone becomes an accurate and fast decoder of English words. And yet, that is exactly what happens! All good readers could quickly and accurately pronounce the made-up words *gand, hade, afuse, sart, malk, lare, jeat, foat, pregal, maw,* and *naul.* Just don't ask them to explain how they did it!

In schools we have traditionally taught students many rules and jargon: the *e* on the end makes the vowel long; vowels in unaccented syllables have a schwa sound; when a vowel is followed by *r*, it is *r* controlled. We have taught so many rules and jargon because it takes over 200 rules to account for the common spelling patterns in English. Although these rules do describe our English alphabetic system, it is doubtful that readers and writers use these rules to decode and spell words. So, how do they do it?

As readers develop some fluency, they decode words by using spelling patterns from the words they know. *Made, fade, blade,* and *shade* all have the same spelling pattern, and the *a* is pronounced the same in all four. When you see the made-up word, *hade,* your mind accesses that known spelling pattern and you give the made-up word the same pronunciation you have for other words with that spelling pattern. Spelling patterns are letters that are commonly seen together in a certain position in words. The *al* at the end of *legal, royal,* and the made-up word *pregal* is a spelling pattern. Sometimes a spelling pattern can be a single letter, as the *a* is in *agree, about, adopt,* and the made-up word *afuse.* Using words you know to decode unknown words is called decoding by analogy.

Spelling patterns are quite reliable indicators of pronunciation—with two exceptions. The first exception was explained in Chapter Six. The most frequently used words are often not pronounced or spelled like other words with that spelling pattern. *To* and *do* should rhyme with *go, so,* and *no. What* should rhyme with *at, cat,* and *bat. They* should be spelled like *way* and *stay. Said* should be spelled like *red* and *bed.* It is precisely because the most frequent words have the least predictable pronunciations and spellings that we use the word wall to help all children learn to read and spell them.

The second exception in spelling patterns is that some spelling patterns have two common sounds. The *ow* at the end of words occurs in *show, grow,* and *slow,* but also in *how, now,* and *cow.* The *ood* at the end of *good, hood,* and *stood* is also found at the end of *food, mood,* and *brood.* Children who are constantly cross-checking meaning with the pronunciations they come up with will not be bothered by these differences, as long as the word they are reading is in their listening-meaning vocabulary.

Whereas spelling patterns work wonderfully well for pronouncing unfamiliar words, they don't work as well for spelling! There are often two or more spelling patterns with the same pronunciation. When trying to read the made-up word *nade,* you would simply compare its pronunciation to other words with that spelling pattern—*made, grade, blade.* If, however, I didn't show you *nade,* but rather pronounced it and asked you to spell it, you might compare it to *maid, paid,* and *braid* and spell it n-a-i-d. Most words can be correctly pronounced by comparing them to known spelling patterns. To spell a word correctly, however, you must often choose between two or more possible spelling patterns.

Part Three contains activities that will help children use patterns to decode words. In Chapter Seven, you will learn how Making Words can help all levels of children move forward in their decoding and spelling abilities. Chapter Eight focuses on rhyming patterns with a variety of activities you can use to teach children to decode and spell using patterns. Once children are decoding and spelling based on patterns, we help them develop their visual checking system and decide which pattern is the correct spelling. Chapter Nine presents two activities—Word Sorting and Hunting and What Looks Right?—to help children become sensitive to spelling patterns. The final section in Chapter Nine describes how all the decoding and spelling activities are multilevel.

chapter 7

Making Words

Making Words (Cunningham & Cunningham, 1992; Cunningham, 2000) is a very popular activity with both teachers and children. Children love manipulating letters to make words and figuring out the secret word that can be made with all the letters. While children are having fun making words, they are also learning important information about phonics and spelling. As children manipulate the letters to make the words, they learn how small changes, such as changing just one letter or moving the letters around, result in completely new words. Children learn to stretch out words and listen for the sounds they hear and the order of those sounds. When you change the first letter, you also change the sound you hear at the beginning of the word. Likewise, when you change the last letter, you change the sound you hear at the end of the word. These ideas seem commonplace and obvious to those of us who have been reading and writing for almost as long as we can remember. But they are a revelation to many beginners—a revelation that gives them tremendous independence in and power over the challenge of decoding and spelling words.

Making Words lessons are an example of a type of instruction called Guided Discovery. In order to truly learn and retain strategies, children must discover them. But some children do not seem to make discoveries about words very easily on their own. In a Making Words lesson, we guide them toward those discoveries by carefully sequencing the words they are to make and giving them explicit guidance about how much change is needed. (See Figure 7.1.)

Making Words lessons have three parts. In the first part, we make words. We begin with short, easy words and move to longer, more complex words. The last word is always the secret word—a word that can be made with all the letters. As children make the words, a child who has it made successfully goes up to the pocket chart or chalk ledge and makes the word with big letters. Children who don't have the word made correctly quickly fix their word to be ready for the next word. The small changes between most words encourage even those children who have not made a word perfectly to fix it because they soon realize that having the current word correctly spelled increases their chances of spelling the next word correctly. In each lesson we make 9–15 words including the secret word that can be made with all the letters. When it is time to make the secret word, we give children one minute to try to come up with the word. After one minute, if no one has discovered the secret word, we give them clues that allow them to figure it out.

In Part Two of a Making Words lesson, we sort the words into patterns. Many children discover patterns just through making the words in the carefully sequenced order, but some children need more explicit guidance. This guidance happens when all the words have been made and teachers guide children to sort them into patterns. Depending on the sophistication of the children and the words available in the lesson, words might be sorted according to their beginning letters—all the letters up to the vowel. Alternatively, to focus on just one sound–letter combination, teachers may ask children to sort out all the words that start with *qu, br,* or *sh.* Once the words with these letters are sorted, the teacher and children pronounce the words and discover that most words that have the same letters also have the same sounds—an important discovery for all emerging readers and writers.

Another pattern children need to discover is that many words have the same root word. If they can pronounce and spell the root word and if they recognize root words with ending, prefixes, or suffixes added, they are able to decode and spell many additional words. To some children, every new word they meet is a new experience! They fail to recognize how new words are related to already known words and, thus, are in the difficult—if not impossible—position of starting from "scratch" and just trying to learn and remember every new word. To be fluent, fast, automatic decoders and spellers, children must learn that *play, playing, played, plays, player,* and *replay* have *play* as their root and use their knowledge of how to decode and spell *play* to quickly transfer to these related words. Whenever possible from the letters available, Making Words lessons include related words. We tell the children that people are related by blood and words are related by meaning. We ask the children to find any related words and sort them out and then we create sentences to show how these words are related.

1. Place the large letter cards needed in a pocket chart or along the chalk tray.

2. Have children pass out letters or pick up the letters needed.

3. Hold up and name the letters on the large letter cards and have the children hold up their matching small letter cards.

4. Write the number 2 (or 3 if there are no two-letter words in this lesson) on the board. Tell them to take two letters and make the first word. Have them say the word after you, stretching out the word to hear all the sounds.

5. Have a child who has the first word made correctly make the same word with the large letter cards on the chalk tray or pocket chart. Do not wait for everyone to make the word before sending someone to make the word with the big letters. Encourage anyone who didn't make the word correctly at first to fix the word when they see it made correctly.

6. Continue to make words, giving students clues such as "Change just the first letter" or "Move the same letters around and you can make a different word" or "Take all your letters out and make another word." Send a child who has the word made correctly to make that word with the large letter cards. Cue them when they need to use more letters by changing the number on the board to indicate the number of letters needed.

7. Before telling them the last word, ask, "Has anyone figured out the secret word we can make with all our letters?" If so, congratulate them and have them make it. If not, say something like, "I love it when I can stump you." Give them clues to help them figure out the big word.

8. Once all the words have been made, take the index cards on which you wrote the words and place them one at a time (in the order made) in the pocket chart or along the chalk tray. Have the children say and spell the words with you as you do this. Use these words for sorting and pointing out patterns. Pick a word and point out a particular spelling pattern—beginning letters, endings, related words, and rhymes. Ask children to find the others with that same pattern. Line these words up so that the pattern is visible.

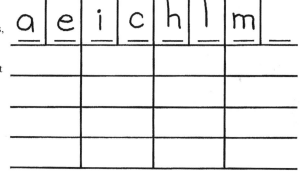

9. To encourage transfer to reading and writing, show students how rhyming words can help them decode and spell other words. Write two words on index cards and have students put these two new words with the rhyming words and use the rhyming words to decode them. Finally, say two words that rhyme, and have students spell these words by deciding which words they rhyme with.

10. If you like, give them a take-home sheet with the same letters across the top (alphabetical order, vowels then consonants, so as not to reveal the secret word to parents). Have the children write capitals on the back, cut the letters apart, and make words to fill the boxes, including words made in class and others they can think of. Here is a sample for a lesson in which the secret word is Michael.

FIGURE 7.1
Steps in Teaching a Making Words Lesson

Source: Cunningham, P. M., Hall, D. P., & Sigmon, C. M. (1999). *The teacher's guide to the four blocks.* Greensboro, NC: Carson-Dellosa. Used with permission from Carson-Dellosa Publishing Company's CD-2406, The Teacher's Guide to the Four Blocks.

In every lesson, we sort the rhyming words. Each lesson contains several sets of rhyming words. Children need to recognize that words that have the same spelling pattern from the vowel to the end of the word usually rhyme. When we sort the words into rhyming words and notice that the words that rhyme have the same spelling pattern, children learn rhyming patterns and how to use words they know to decode and spell lots of other words.

The final part of a Making Words lesson is the transfer step. All the working and playing with words we do while making words are worth nothing if children do not use what they know when they need to use it. Many children know letter sounds and patterns and do not apply these to decode an unknown word encountered during reading or spell a word they need while writing. All teachers know that it is much easier to teach children phonics than it is to actually get them to use it. This is the reason that we end every Making Words lesson with a transfer step. Once we have the words sorted according to rhyme, we tell children to pretend they are reading and come to a new word. As we say this, we write a word that has the same spelling pattern and rhymes with one set of rhyming words. We show this word to a child and ask that child to come up and put the new word with the words it rhymes with. We don't allow anyone to say the new word until it is lined up under the other rhyming words, and then we lead the children to pronounce the rhyming words they made and the new word. We then show them one more word, which we ask a child to:

> "Pretend you're reading and come to this new word. Put it with the words
> that would help you figure it out."

Once we have decoded two new words using the rhyming patterns from the words we made, we help the children transfer their letter–sound knowledge to writing. To do this, we ask children to pretend they are writing and need to spell a word:

> "Pretend you're writing and you need to spell the word *stray.* You stretch out
> *stray* and hear the beginning letters *str.* If you can think of the words we made
> today that rhyme with *stray,* you will have the correct spelling of the word."

The children decide that *stray* rhymes with the *ay* words they made and that *stray* is spelled *s-t-r-a-y.* We finish the lesson by having them spell one more word by deciding which of the words they made it rhymes with.

A Sample Making Words Lesson

As the person who is teaching the lesson, the teacher is always the best person to decide exactly what to say to children and how to cue them about the different words. If you have a child in your class named *Gail,* you will cue them differently than a teacher who does not have a *Gail.* Your children will relate better to example sentences you come up with that relate to the communities and lives of your children. With the caveat that you can do this much better for your children than I—who have never seen your children—here is a sample that you can use to construct your own lesson cues.

Beginning the Lesson

The children all have the letters: *a, e, i, d, f, g, l,* and *r.* These same letters—big enough for all to see—are displayed in a pocket chart or along the chalk ledge. The vowels are in a different color from the other letters and the letter cards have lowercase letters on one side and capital letters on the other.

The teacher has written the words the children are going to make on index cards. These will be placed in the pocket chart as the words are made and will be used for the sort and transfer steps of the lesson.

The teacher begins the lesson by having each child hold up and name each letter as the teacher holds up the big letters in the pocket chart.

> "Hold up and name each letter as I hold up the big letter. Let's start with your vowels. Show me your *a;* your *e;* and your *i.* Now show me your *d, f, g, l,* and *r.* You all have eight letters. In a few minutes, we will see if anyone can figure out the secret word that uses all eight letters. Make sure all your letters are showing their lowercase side to start with. When we are making a name, I will cue you and look to see who remembers to turn the first letter in that name to the capital side. Let's get started making words."

Part One: Making Words

> "Use three letters to spell the word *die.* My puppy was sick, but fortunately, he didn't *die.*"

Find someone with *die* spelled correctly and send that child to spell *die* with the big letters.

> "Change just one letter and turn *die* into *lie.* It is wrong to tell a *lie.*"
>
> "Start over and use three letters to spell *age.* My mom says it is not polite to ask people their *age.*"

Quickly send someone with the correct spelling to the big letters. Keep the pace brisk. Do not wait until everyone has *age* spelled with their little letters. It is fine if some children are making *age* as *age* is being spelled with the big letters.

> "Make sure you have *age* spelled correctly. Add just one letter to spell *rage.* When they guessed his name, Rumpelstiltskin flew into a *rage.*"

Continue sending children to make the words with the big letters. Remind children to use the big letters to check what they have made with their letters, fixing their own word as needed before going on to the next word. Move the lesson along at a fast pace.

> "Start over and use four letters to spell *lied.* The suspect *lied* about where he was at the time of the robbery."
>
> "Start over and use four letters to spell *fail.* I was glad I didn't *fail* the test."
>
> "Change one letter to spell the name *Gail.* We read a story about a girl named *Gail.*"
>
> "Use four letters to spell *fire.* The fire truck raced to the *fire.*"
>
> "Add one letter to spell *fired.* My cousin was *fired* from his job."
>
> "Use the same letters in *fired* to spell *fried.* We caught some fish and *fried* it."
>
> "Start over and use five letters to spell *grade.* What *grade* is your sister in?"
>
> "Use the same letters in *grade* to spell *raged.* The wind blew and the fire *raged.*"
>
> "Start over and use five letters to spell *field.* We met at the soccer *field.*"
>
> "I have just one word left. It is the secret word you can make with all your letters. See if you can figure it out."

(Give them one minute to figure out the secret word and then give clues if needed.)

> "Our secret word today is a name that you can spell by adding your letters to *field.*"

Let someone go to the big letters and spell the secret word—*Garfield.*

Let all the children make the word *Garfield* and talk about anyone named *Garfield* that they know. Many children may know *Garfield,* the cat.

Part Two: Sorting the Words into Patterns

Have the children read aloud with you all the words made in the lesson. Then have them sort out the related words. Remind the children that related words share a root word and some meaning. When the words are sorted, have children make sentences using both related words in the same sentence.

Next sort out the rhyming words. Send several children to the pocket chart to find rhyming words with the same pattern and line these up with rhymes one under the other.

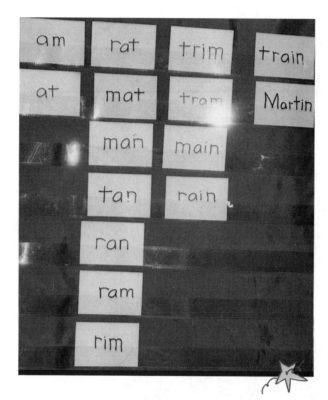

These words were made in a Making Words lesson in which the secret word was *Martin.*

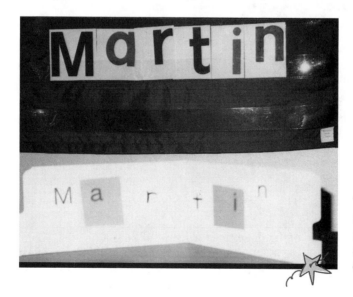

The secret word was made with the big pocket-chart letters and in one of the children's holders.

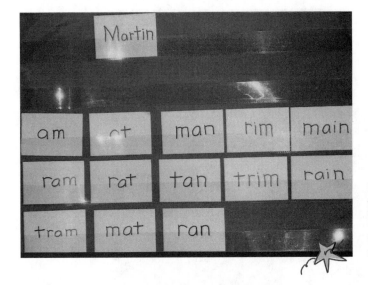

In the second part of the Making Words lesson, the words are sorted according to rhymes.

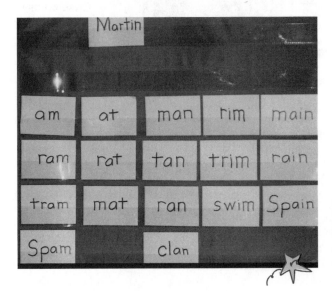

At the end of the Making Words lesson, the transfer words *Spam, clan, swim,* and *Spain* are displayed in the pocket chart.

Part Three: Transfer

Tell the children to pretend they are reading and they come to a new word. Show one child the word *wage* written on an index card. Let that child put **wage** under **rage** and **age** and have all the children pronounce all three words, using the rhyming words they made to decode the new word *wage*. Do the same thing with *frail*.

Next, tell the children to pretend they are writing and need to spell a word.

"Let's pretend Joey is writing and he is trying to spell the word *tie.*"

Have the children tell you that *tie* begins with *t* and write *t* on an index card. Then have the children pronounce the sets of rhyming words in the pocket chart and decide that *tie* rhymes with **die** and **lie,** and use the *i-e* pattern to finish spelling *tie.* Do the same thing with *stage.*

When you finish the lesson, the rhyming words you made will be lined up in the pocket chart along with two new words they helped you read and two new words they helped you spell.

Making Words Homework

Because students like to manipulate the letters and come up with their own words, we usually give them a take-home sheet with the same letters used in the lesson. The sheet has the letters across the top and blocks for writing words. Students write capital letters on the back and then cut the letters apart. They manipulate the letters to make words and then write them in the blocks. This is a popular homework assignment with students and their parents. When we write the letters at the top, we write them in alphabetical order—vowels and then consonants—so as not to give away the secret word. Before children take the sheet home, we have them turn it over and write the capital letters on the back. Children love being the "smart" ones who "know the secret word" and watching parents and other relatives try to figure it out.

Additional Making Words Lessons

Here are some lessons to get you started. More lessons can be found in the books referenced at the end of this chapter. *Making Names* (Cunningham, 2004) includes

Systematic Sequential Phonics (Cunningham, 2000) contains a series of Making Words lessons that follows a traditional phonics sequence. Lessons are available in "paper" format from Carson-Dellosa. These same lessons are also available on the computer in Word Maker published by Don Johnston. Children can access these lessons on the computer and work through them individually at their own pace.

1. Decide upon a "secret word" which can be made with all the letters. In choosing this word, consider child interest, the curriculum tie-ins you can make, and the letter/sound patterns to which you can draw children's attention through the sorting at the end.

2. Make a list of other words that can be made from these letters.

3. From all the words you could make, pick 12–15 words using these criteria:

   • Words that you can sort for the pattern you want to emphasize.

   • Little words and big words so that the lesson is a multilevel lesson (Making the little words helps your struggling students; making the big words challenges your highest-achieving students).

   • "Abracadabra" words that can be made with the same letters in different places (**side/dies**) so children are reminded that, when words are spelled, the order of the letters is crucial.

   • A proper name or two to remind students to use capital letters.

   • Words that most students have in their listening vocabularies.

4. Write all the words on index cards and order them from shortest to longest.

5. Once you have the two-letter, three-letter, etc., words together, order them so you can emphasize letter patterns and show how changing the position of the letters, changing one letter, or adding one letter results in a different word.

6. Choose some letters or patterns by which to sort.

7. Choose four transfer words—uncommon words you can read and spell based on the rhyming words.

8. Store the cards in an envelope. On the envelope, write the words in order, the patterns for which you will sort, and the transfer words.

FIGURE 7.2
Steps in Planning a Making Words Lesson

Source: Cunningham, P. M., & Hall, D. P. (1998). *Month-by-month phonics for third grade.* Greensboro, NC: Carson-Dellosa. Used with permission from Carson-Dellosa Publishing Company's CD-2404, Month-by-Month Phonics for Third Grade.

lessons for 210 popular children's names. Also see Figure 7.2 for steps in planning a Making Words lesson.

One-Vowel Lessons

One-vowel lessons are a great way to start the year. Be sure to have your children stretch out the words and listen for all the letters before making them.

blast   1. Make: *al as at sat bat tab stab/bats last blast* (Words separated by / can be made with the same letters.)

2. Sort beginning letters
   Sort rhymes: *at, sat, bat; tab, stab; last, blast*

3. Transfer: *past, fat; cab, fast*

string   1. Make: *is in it sit rig ring/grin sing sting string*

2. Sort beginning letters
   Sort rhymes: *it, sit; in, grin; sing, sting, string*

3. Transfer: *swing, fit; spin, win*

trunks   1. Make: *us sun run rut nut nuts/stun rust trunk trunks*

2. Sort beginning letters
   Sort rhymes: *sun, run, stun; rut, nut*

3. Transfer: *stun, hut; cut, spun*

spent   1. Make: *pen ten/net pet pest/pets nets/nest/sent spent*

2. Sort beginning letters
   Sort rhymes: *pen, ten; net, pet; pest, nest; pets, nets; sent, spent*

3. Transfer: *test, tent; jets, west*

ponds   1. Make: *so no/on Don nod pod pods nods pond ponds*

2. Sort beginning letters
   Sort rhymes: *so, no; on, Don; nod, pod; pods, nods*

3. Transfer: *rod, rods; Ron, Bo*

Theme/Holiday Lessons

valentines 1. Make: *an van vet vent vest nest sent vine base valentines*

2. Sort *v* words: *van, vet, vent, vest, vine, valentines*
   Sort rhymes: *an, van; sent, vent; nest, vest*

3. Transfer: *bent, chest; spent, west*

elephants   1. Make: *pet pest past last east least sheep sleep asleep please elephants*

2. Sort related words: *sleep, asleep*
   Sort rhymes: *past, last; sleep, sheep, asleep; east, least*

3. Transfer: *beast, blast; steep, feast*

football   1. Make: *to too all fall ball tall tool fool foot football*

2. Sort related words: *foot, ball, football*
   Sort rhymes: *all, fall, ball, tall; tool, fool*

3. Transfer: *school, stall; mall, stool*

dancers   1. Make: *an can car cars/scar care dare dance scare scared dancers*

2. Sort related words: *scare, scared; dance, dancers*
   Sort rhymes: *an, can; car, scar, dare, care, scare*

3. Transfer: *plan, stare; scan, par*

teacher   1. Make: *at cat eat ear hear heat each reach teach/cheat there
   teacher/cheater*

2. Sort related words: *teach, teacher; cheat, cheater*
   Sort rhymes: *at, cat; eat, heat, cheat; reach, each, teach; ear, hear*

3. Transfer: *spear, peach; beach, treat*

Lessons with Children's Names

Alexander   1. Make: *Ed Ned Rex and land Alan Alex lead/deal real relax
   leader/dealer relaxed Alexander*

2. Sort related words: *lead, leader; deal, dealer; relax, relaxed*
   Sort rhymes: *and, land; deal, real*

3. Transfer: *squeal, stand; steal, grand*

Barney   1. Make: *ear Ray bay ban ran bran/barn yarn year near earn yearn
   Barney*

2. Sort beginning letters
   Sort rhymes: *Ray, bay; ban, ran, bran; barn, yarn; ear, year, near;
   earn, yearn*

3. Transfer: *learn, clear; stray; clan*

Clifford   1. Make: *of off for old oil coil foil Lori cold fold Ford cord Cliff Clifford*

2. Sort beginning letters
   Sort rhymes: *old, cold, fold; Ford, cord; oil, coil, foil*

3. Transfer: *told, boil; broil, scold*

Technology Tip

To make planning your own lessons quick and easy, go to www.wordplays.com and click on Words in a Word. Type in the secret word and immediately you will have all the words (excluding proper names) you can make from these letters. Pick and choose those that will suit your lesson goals and make the lesson multilevel.

Dorothy   1. Make: *hot rot Rod Roy try dry toy hood hoot root Troy door/odor*
                       Dorothy

            2. Sort beginning letters
               Sort rhymes: *hot, rot; Roy, Troy; hoot, root; try, dry*

            3. Transfer: *boot, sky; shoot, shot*

Frederick   1. Make: *kid rid Eric Fred Rick Dick fire fired/fried cried/cider rider*
                         Derrick Frederick

             2. Sort related words: *fire, fired*
                Sort rhymes: *kid, rid; fried, cried; rider, cider*

             3. Transfer: *tried, spider; slid, spied*

Brianna   1. Make: *in an Ian ran ban Nan Anna rain barn/bran brain/Brian*
                       Brianna

           2. Sort br words: *bran, brain, Brian, Brianna*
              Sort rhymes: *an, ran, ban, bran, Nan; rain, brain*

           3. Transfer: *Spain, span; clan, chain*

 Summary

Making Words is a favorite activity of many children. You can pick the secret word to go with a unit you are studying, a story you have read, a phonics skill you want to emphasize, or an interesting-to-your-children name. Each lesson includes 9–15 words that will make a multilevel lesson with short, easy words at the beginning and more complex words at the end. Be sure to include some rhyming words for the sort and transfer steps. If there are several words that begin with particular letter combinations you want to emphasize, include them so that you can sort them and notice the letters and sounds. When related words occur, include them and sort for these to help children begin to realize how you decode and spell longer words by recognizing the root word and endings.

chapter 8

Rhyme-Based Decoding and Spelling Activities

Making Words lessons do focus on rhyme during the sort and transfer steps. They also focus children's attention on single letters as they process the letters sequentially to spell the words. In addition to Making Words, there are many other activities that help children focus on and learn rhyming patterns that help them decode and spell thousands of words. In this chapter, you will learn how to do Rounding Up the Rhymes, Using Words You Know, and Reading/Writing Rhymes activities to help children learn and use rhyming patterns.

Learning the Most Common Rhyming Patterns

As children are learning the beginning sounds and how they can use these sounds to figure out words, they should also be learning some

Here are the 37 high-frequency spelling patterns (with possible key words):

ack (black)	ap (cap)	est (nest)	ing (king)	ot (hot)
ail (pail)	ash (trash)	ice (rice)	ink (pink)	uck (truck)
ain (train)	at (cat)	ide (bride)	ip (ship)	ug (bug)
ake (cake)	ate (skate)	ick (brick)	it (hit)	ump (jump)
ale (whale)	aw (claw)	ight (night)	ock (sock)	unk (skunk)
ame (game)	ay (tray)	ill (hill)	oke (Coke)	
an (pan)	eat (meat)	in (pin)	op (mop)	
ank (bank)	ell (shell)	ine (nine)	ore (store)	

of the most common rhyming patterns. These rhyming patterns are called *rimes* by linguists and often called *word families* or *phonograms* by teachers. We call them *spelling patterns* because we want children to learn that you spell based on patterns—which includes the vowel and the letters that follow. Thirty-seven spelling patterns allow children to read and spell over 500 words commonly used by young children (Wylie & Durrell, 1970). Many teachers display these with a word and picture to help children learn the patterns that help them spell many other words.

In addition, there are numerous books teachers can read to children and then children can read on their own that contain lots of examples of rhyming words with these most common rhyming patterns. Books with just one rhyming pattern in which almost all the words have the same spelling pattern are the most helpful for children just learning patterns and how they help you spell words. C. and J. Hawkins have written four of these books: *Tog the Dog* (1986), *Jen the Hen* (1985), *Mig the Pig* (1984), and *Pat the Cat* (1993). Rigby publishes a set of Kinderrhymes with 24 titles, including *Rimes with Cat, Rimes with Cap,* and *Rhymes with King. Zoo Looking* by Mem Fox (1995) has many words that rhyme with *back.*

Other particularly helpful books are ones that contain just 6–8 different rhyming pairs. *There's a Bug in My Mug* and *My Nose Is a Hose,* both by Kent Salisbury (1997), are two such books. Both books contain tabs that when pulled reveal what is in the mug or turn the nose into a hose. These books are great fun and wonderful for helping children begin to understand how rhyming patterns work.

Rounding Up the Rhymes

Rounding Up the Rhymes is an activity to follow up the reading of a book, story, or poem that contains lots of rhyming words. Here is an example using that timeless book, *I Wish That I Had Duck Feet* (Seuss, 1972). The first reading of anything should be for meaning and enjoyment. In Dr. Seuss's *I Wish That I Had Duck Feet*, a boy wishes he had duck feet so that he could splash and wouldn't have to wear shoes until he realizes his mother wouldn't want him in the house like that. The boy goes on to wish for deer horns, a whale spout, a long tail, and a long nose until he thinks of the complications each would cause and finally decides to "be just me." As with so many other Seuss books, this one has enormous appeal for children.

After enjoying the book, point out to the children that in addition to a silly story and great illustrations, Dr. Seuss books are fun to read because of all the rhyming words. Tell the children that you are going to read several pages of *I Wish That I Had Duck Feet* again and they can help you "round up the rhymes." Read the first page and have students help you decide that the rhyming words are **why** and **dry.** Write these words on two index cards and place them one under the other in a pocket chart. Read the next page and have the children identify the rhyming words, **me** and **see.** Continue to read until you have six or seven sets of rhyming words.

why	me	brown	play	floor	don't	instead
dry	see	town	way	door	won't	head

Now, reread these pages again. As you get to the rhyming words, point to them in the pocket chart and have the children say them.

Next, have the children help you identify the spelling pattern. Explain that the spelling pattern in a short word includes all the letters beginning with the first vowel and going to the end of the word. After naming the vowels—*a, e, i, o, u,* and sometimes *y*—pick up the first set of rhyming words **why** and **dry,** have the children tell you the spelling pattern in each, and underline the spelling pattern. In **why** and **dry,** the spelling pattern is only the *y.* Put wh*y* and dr*y* back in the pocket chart and pick up the next set of rhymes—**me** and **see.** Have the children say them and hear once more that they do rhyme. Then underline the spelling patterns: *e* and *ee.* They do rhyme, but they have a different spelling pattern. Explain that we only want to keep rhymes with the same spelling pattern, then toss *me* and *see* in the trash can.

Continue with the remaining pairs, deciding first that they rhyme and then underlining the spelling pattern to see if it is the same. There are now six pairs of rhyming words with the same spelling pattern in the pocket chart:

wh<u>y</u>	br<u>own</u>	pl<u>ay</u>	fl<u>oor</u>	d<u>on't</u>	inst<u>ead</u>
dr<u>y</u>	t<u>own</u>	w<u>ay</u>	d<u>oor</u>	w<u>on't</u>	h<u>ead</u>

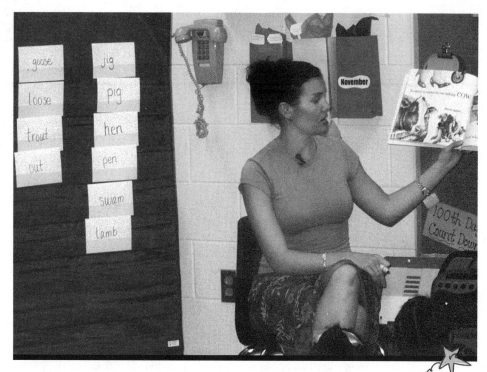

This teacher is rereading a book and the children are telling her the rhyming words. They round up the rhymes in the pocket chart on index cards.

The final part of this activity is the transfer step—how we use rhyming words to read and spell other words. Begin the transfer part of this activity by telling children something like:

> "You know that when you are reading books and writing stories, there are words you have never seen before. You have to figure them out. One way people figure out how to read and spell new words is to see if they already know any rhyming words or words that have the same spelling pattern. I am going to write some words and you can see which words with the same spelling pattern will help you read them. Then we are going to spell some words by deciding which words they rhyme with."

Write two or three words that rhyme and have the same spelling pattern as the words in the pocket chart. Let the children underline the spelling pattern and put each word in the pocket chart under the other words with the same spelling pattern. Help the children use the rhyme to decode the words.

Any book with lots of rhyming words—most of which have the same pattern—is a good candidate for a Rounding Up the Rhymes lesson. Because you will only round up the rhymes from part of the book, you can choose pages on which most of the rhymes have the same spelling pattern. You don't want to throw out more words than you keep! Many teachers tie this activity in with an author study of Dr. Seuss. Some of his other books that work particularly well are *In a People House, Ten Apples Up on Top,* and *One Fish, Two Fish, Red Fish, Blue Fish.* Other great books for Rounding Up the Rhymes include:

Golden Bear, by Ruth Young (Scholastic, 1992)
How I Spent My Summer Vacation, by Mark Teague (Crown, 1995)
Inside, Outside Christmas, by Robin Spowart (Holiday House, 1998)
Penguins Climb, Penguins Rhyme, by Bruce McMillan (Harcourt Brace, 1995)
This Is the Pumpkin, by Abby Levine (Whitman, 1998)
Ten Little Dinosaurs, by Pattie Schnetzler (Accord, 1996)

Finally, say two or three words that rhyme. The children decide what words they rhyme with and use the spelling pattern to spell them. Here are the *I Wish That I Had Duck Feet* words along with the new words read and spelled based on their rhymes and spelling patterns.

wh<u>y</u>	br<u>own</u>	pl<u>ay</u>	f<u>loor</u>	<u>don't</u>	inst<u>ead</u>
dr<u>y</u>	t<u>own</u>	w<u>ay</u>	d<u>oor</u>	w<u>on't</u>	h<u>ead</u>
sk<u>y</u>	cl<u>own</u>	tr<u>ay</u>	p<u>oor</u>		br<u>ead</u>

Using Words You Know

Another activity that helps children learn patterns and how patterns help you read and write is called Using Words You Know. To plan a Using Words You Know lesson, we pick three or four words that our children can read and spell and that have many rhyming words spelled the same way. While about half the word-wall words are irregular words such as *they, was,* and *have,* other words follow the expected pattern. Many teachers put a star on those word-wall words such as *big, play, not, make, ride,* and *thing* that help you spell lots of other words and use these in a Using Words You Know activity. Recently we have begun using some well-known brand names that have lots of rhyming words. We bring in packages with the product names and then use those names as the known words. Children are highly motivated by these products and are fascinated to see how many other words these products can help them read and spell. Here is a sample lesson using ice cream and Cool Whip.

We begin the lesson by displaying the products and letting children talk a little about them. Next we draw their attention to the names and tell them that these names will help them spell and read a lot of other words. Using the board, chart, or overhead, we make columns and head each with one of the key words, underlining the spelling pattern. The students do the same on a sheet of paper. At the beginning of the lesson, their papers look like this:

ice   cr<u>eam</u>   c<u>ool</u>   wh<u>ip</u>

We then show them words that rhyme with *ice, cream, cool,* or *whip.* We do not say these words and do not allow them to say the words but rather have them write them in the column with the same spelling pattern. We send one child to write the word on the chart, board, or overhead. When everyone has the word written under the word that will help them read it, we have them say the known word and the rhyming word. We help them to verbalize the strategy they are using by saying something like,

> "If *c-r-e-a-m* is *cream, d-r-e-a-m* must be *dream.* If *c-o-o-l* is *cool, d-r-o-o-l* is *drool.*"

After showing them 8–10 words and having them use the known word to decode them, we help them practice using known words to spell unknown words. To help them spell, we can't show them a word. Rather, we say a word, such as *twice,* and have them say the word and write it under the word that it rhymes with. Again, we help them verbalize their strategy by leading them to explain,

> "If *ice* is spelled *i-c-e, twice* is probably spelled *t-w-i-c-e.* If *whip* is spelled *w-h-i-p, strip* is probably spelled *s-t-r-i-p.*"

Here are what the children's sheets might look like when all the one-syllable rhyming words have been added:

<u>ice</u>	cr<u>eam</u>	c<u>ool</u>	wh<u>ip</u>
nice	dream	drool	tip
mice	stream	pool	skip
slice	scream	fool	trip
twice	gleam	spool	strip
dice	beam	stool	clip

To make the lesson a bit more multilevel and show children that decoding and spelling based on rhyming words work for bigger words too, we would end the lesson by showing them a few longer words and having them write them under the rhymes and use the rhymes to decode them. Finally, we would say a few longer words, help them with the spelling of the first syllables, and have them use the rhyme to spell the last syllable. Here is what their papers would look like with some added longer words:

ice	cream	cool	whip
nice	dream	drool	tip
mice	stream	pool	skip
slice	scream	fool	trip
twice	gleam	spool	strip
dice	beam	stool	clip
sacrifice	mainstream	whirlpool	equip
device	downstream	preschool	spaceship

It is very important for Using Words You Know lessons (and the transfer step of Rounding Up the Rhymes and Making Words lessons) that you choose the rhyming words for them to read and spell rather than ask them for rhyming words. In English, there are often two spelling patterns for the same rhyme. If you ask them what rhymes with *cream* or *cool,* they may come up with words with the *e-e-m* pattern such as *seem* and words with the *u-l-e* pattern such as *rule.* The fact that there are two common patterns for many rhymes does not hinder us while reading. When we see the word *drool,* our brain thinks of other *o-o-l* words such as *cool* and *school.* We make this new word *drool* rhyme with *cool* and *school* and then check out this pronunciation with the meaning of whatever we are reading. If we were going to write the word *drool* for the first time, we wouldn't know for sure which spelling pattern to use, and we might think of the rhyming word *rule* and use that pattern. Spelling requires both a sense of word patterns and a visual checking sense. When you write a word and then think, "That doesn't look right!" and then write it using a different pattern, you are demonstrating that you have developed a visual checking sense. Once children become good at spelling by pattern—rather than putting down one letter for each sound, we help them develop their visual checking sense through two activities: Reading/Writing Rhymes and What Looks Right? During Using Words You Know lessons, we are trying to get them to spell based on pattern, and we "finesse" the problem of two patterns by choosing the words we present to them.

Using Words You Know lessons are easy to plan if you use a good rhyming dictionary. We use the *Scholastic Rhyming Dictionary* (Young, 1994). Children enjoy Using Words You Know, especially if the words you use are popular products such as *Coke, Crest, Tang,* and *Cat Chow.*

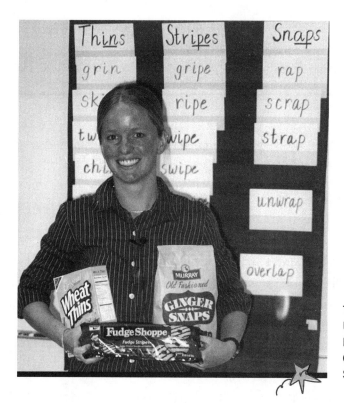

This teacher is doing a Using Words You Know lesson using Wheat Thins, Ginger Snaps, and Fudge Stripes.

Steps in Teaching a Using Words You Know Lesson

1. Display and talk about the words children know.
2. Make as many columns as needed on the board and on student papers. Head these with the known word and underline the spelling pattern.
3. Show one-syllable words written on index cards. Have them write them under the word with the same pattern and use the rhyme to pronounce the words.
4. Say one-syllable words and have them decide how to spell them by deciding which word they rhyme with.
5. Repeat the preceding procedure with longer words.
6. Help students explain how words they know help them read and spell lots of other words, including longer words.

Here are some sample lessons using popular products and places.

Products: <u>B</u><u>old</u>   <u>Sh</u><u>out</u>   <u>Ch</u><u>eer</u>

One-syllable words to read: *sold, scout, told, deer, mold, shout, clout, trout, peer, steer*

One-syllable words to spell: *gold, pout, spout, sprout, jeer, sneer, cold, scold, stout, fold*

Longer words to read: *checkout, reindeer, blackout, blindfold, scaffold, knockout, uphold, dropout, engineer*

Longer words to spell: *cookout, without, household, handout, unfold, fallout, withhold, pioneer, volunteer*

Products: <u>K</u><u>it</u> <u>K</u><u>at</u> <u>G</u><u>old</u> <u>F</u><u>ish</u>

One-syllable words to read: *spit, split, that, grit, flat, dish, bold, spat, mold, rat*

One-syllable words to spell: *slit, old, hold, wish, swish, quit, chat, hat, hit, brat*

Longer words to read: *admit, profit, misfit, wildcat, credit, Democrat, selfish, unselfish, acrobat, blindfold*

Longer words to spell: *permit, visit, combat, outfit, nonfat, catfish, starfish, billfold, doormat*

Products: <u>K</u><u>ool</u> <u>Aid</u>   <u>P</u><u>op</u> <u>C</u><u>orn</u>

One-syllable words to read: *horn, cop, raid, worn, drop, maid, prop, fool, shop, born*

One-syllable words to spell: *torn, flop, braid, scorn, crop, thorn, tool, stool, paid, chop*

Longer words to read: *mermaid, lollipop, unicorn, stillborn, workshop, bridesmaid, prepaid, toadstool*

Longer words to spell: *newborn, unpaid, raindrop, gumdrop, acorn, afraid, nonstop, stepstool*

Places: Taco B<u>ell</u>   Burger K<u>ing</u>   Pizza H<u>ut</u>

One-syllable words to read: *fell, part, shut, bring, yell, sting, string, shell, sell, rut, quell, fling*

One-syllable words to spell: *ring, spring, swell, wing, swing, smell, strut, glut, spell, well*

Longer words to read: *haircut, misspell, firststring, darling, inning, peanut, dumbbell*

Longer words to spell: *retell, shortcut, seashell, something, hamstring, upswing, undercut*

Reading/Writing Rhymes

Reading/Writing Rhymes is another activity that helps students learn to use patterns to decode and spell hundreds of words. In addition all beginning letters (onsets) are reviewed every time you do a Reading/Writing Rhymes lesson. Once all the rhyming words are generated on a chart, students write rhymes using these words and then read each other's rhymes. Because writing and reading are connected to every lesson, students learn how to use these patterns as they actually read and write. Here is how to do Reading/Writing Rhymes lessons.

The Onset Deck

You will need an onset deck containing cards for all the beginning sounds. The cards, 3×5 index cards, are laminated and have the single-letter consonants written in blue, the blends in red, and the digraphs and other two-letter combinations in green. On one side of each card, the first letter of the onset is a capital letter. The onset deck contains 50 beginning letter cards including:

Single consonants: *b c d f g h j k l m n p r s t v w y z*

Digraphs (two letters, one sound): *sh ch wh th*

Other two-letter, one-sound combinations: *kn qu*

Blends (beginning letters blended together, sometimes called clusters): *bl br cl cr dr fl fr gl gr pl pr sc scr sk sl sm sn sp spl spr st str sw tr tw*

At the beginning of the lesson, we distribute all the onset cards to the students. Depending on your class, you can distribute them to individual children or to teams of two or three children.

Making the Chart of Rhyming Words

Once all the onset cards are distributed, we write the spelling pattern we are working with 10–12 times on a piece of chart paper or a transparency as in Figure 8.1. As we write it each time, we have the children help spell it and pronounce it.

Next, we invite all the children who think they have a card that makes a real word to line up next to the chart or overhead. As each child shows his or her card, we blend the onset and the rhyming pattern together to decide if the word is a real word. If the word is indeed a real word, we use the word in a sentence and write that word on the chart. If the word is not a real word, we explain why we cannot write it on the chart. (If a word is a real word and does rhyme but has a different spelling pattern, such as *plaid* to rhyme with *ad,* we explain that it rhymes but has a different pattern and

ad

_____ ad	_____ ad
_____ ad	_____ ad
_____ ad	_____ ad
_____ ad	_____
_____ ad	_____
_____ ad	_____
_____ ad	_____
_____ ad	

_____

*

granddad   undergrad   Conrad

FIGURE 8.1
**A Transparency
Ready to Be Used
in an** *-ad* **Reading/
Writing Rhymes
Lesson**

include it on the bottom of the chart with an asterisk next to it.) We write names with capital letters and, if a word can be a name and not a name, such as *tad* and *Tad,* we write it both ways. When all the children who think they can spell words with their beginning letters and the spelling pattern have come up, we call children up to make the words not yet there by saying something like,

"I think the person with the *f* card could come up here and add *f* to *ad* to make a word we know."

We try to include all the words that any of our children would have in their listening vocabulary, but we avoid obscure words. If the patterns we wrote to begin our chart get made into complete words, we add as many more as needed. Finally, if we can think of some good longer words that rhyme and have that spelling pattern, we add them to the list. (We spell and write the whole word here since children do not have the extra letters needed to spell it.)

Writing Sentences with the Rhyming Words

Once the chart of rhyming words is written, we work together in a shared writing format to write a couple of sentences using lots of the rhyming words.

Next the students write rhymes. Many teachers put them in teams to write these rhymes and then let them read their rhymes to the class.

You can use the Reading/Writing Rhymes format to teach any of the common vowel patterns. If you are using a basal reader or curriculum guide that specifies an order in which the vowel sounds will be taught and tested, let that guide determine the order in which you make charts for Reading/Writing Rhymes. Just as for Using Words You Know, we use a rhyming dictionary as our source for the rhyming words. We pick the patterns that have the most rhyming examples. (Some patterns will generate some "bad" words. You can either not distribute the beginning letters that would make the "bad" words or tell children that there are some words that could be made that "we never use in school" so we won't include them. And you don't need anyone to tell you what they are!)

Reading/Writing Rhymes with Two or More Spelling Patterns

Some rhymes have two common spelling patterns. If you are reading and come to the new word *blight*, you can easily use the *ight* pattern to decode it. If you come to the word *cite*, you can use the *ite* pattern to decode it. But, if you need to spell a word that rhymes with *tight* and *bite*, which spelling pattern should you use? We use Reading/ Writing Rhymes lessons to sensitize children to the different spelling patterns some rhymes share.

A Two-Pattern Lesson

When spelling a word, there is no way to know which one is the correct spelling unless you recognize it as a word you know after writing it. (This is why we often write a word and think "that doesn't look right," and then try writing it with the other pattern to see if that looks right.) When we write rhymes that have two common spelling patterns, we write both patterns on the same chart.

Students come up and tell us the word their beginning letters will make and we write it with the correct pattern. In many cases, there are two homophones, words that are spelled differently and have different meanings but the same pronunciation. We write both of these and talk about what each one means. (Artistic teachers sometimes draw a little picture next to one of these so that students can tell them apart.) See Figure 8.2 for the *ail/ale* long vowel spelling pattern.

-ail/-ale

_____ail	_____ale
_____ail	_____ale
_____ail	_____ale
_____ail	_____ale
_____ail	_____ale
_____ail	_____ale
_____ail	_____ale
_____ail	_____ale

*_____

Abigail   detail   female   tattletale

FIGURE 8.2
A Transparency Ready to Be Used in an -*ail*/*ale* Reading/Writing Rhymes Lesson

Just as in the single-pattern lessons, we let children help us by coming up with a couple of silly sentences and write these on the board.

Children then write a few silly sentences of their own.

A Reading/Writing Rhymes lesson usually ends with volunteers reading their silly sentences aloud to the class or group.

Vowel Patterns for Reading/ Writing Rhymes Lessons

All the common vowel patterns can be taught through Reading/Writing Rhymes. Here are the vowel patterns that are common enough to merit teaching and make good Reading/Writing Rhymes lessons:

Rhymes with only one common spelling pattern

ack	ad	am	an	ap	ash	at	ake	ar	ark	art
ay	aw	ank	ang							
ell	en	et								
ick	ip	ill	it	in	ice	ine	ing	ink		
op	ot	ock	ob	orn	ook	oom	oy	oil	out	
ug	ut	ump	unch							

Rhymes with two or more common patterns

ail/ale	ain/ane	ait/ate	ace/ase	and/anned
ants/ance	aste/aced	ax/acks	ays/aze	
ed/ead	est/essed	ead/eed	eak/eek	eal/eel
eap/eep	eat/eet			
ide/ied	ite/ight	ix/icks		
oak/oke	oat/ote	old/olled	oot/ute	
e/ea/ee	o/oe/ow	ade/aid/ayed	oan/one/own	
oal/ole/oll	ool/ule/uel	un/on/one		
are/air/ear	ear/eer/ere	ert/irt/urt	urn/ern/earn	ore/oar/oor/our
all/awl/aul	ew/ue/oo	y/igh/ie	ary/airy/erry/arry	ees/eas/ease/eeze

Transparencies for doing Reading/Writing Rhymes lessons are available from Carson-Dellosa. *Reading/Writing Simple Rhymes* (Cunningham & Hall, 2003) has rhymes with just one common spelling pattern. *Reading/Writing Complex Rhymes* (Cunningham & Hall, 2003) has rhymes with two or more common spelling patterns.

Summary

All the activities in this chapter help focus children's attention on rhyming patterns and how these rhyming patterns (rimes) help them decode and spell words. As children engage in the activities, they are constantly reviewing all the beginning letters (onsets) as they combine these with the rimes to figure out words. All the activities emphasize transfer. Most teachers know that it is much easier to teach children phonics than it is to actually have them use phonics when they need to figure out how to decode a new word while reading or spell a new word while writing. Rounding Up the Rhymes facilitates transfer because the rhymes are from books and children are, thus, more apt to recall this strategy when reading other books. The transfer step of Rounding Up the Rhymes is exactly the same as the transfer step in Making Words.

> "Pretend you are reading and come to this word. Put it with the words it rhymes with and blend the beginning sounds and rhyme to decode it."

> "Pretend you are writing and you need to spell *clown*. Stretch *clown* out to hear the beginning letters and then use the rhyming pattern from the rhymes we rounded up."

Using Words You Know shows children explicitly how all the words they know, including interesting "brand names," can help them decode and spell other less familiar words. In Reading/Writing Rhymes, children blend onsets and rimes together to decode words. They then immediately transfer those rhyming words into their writing by composing some silly sentences. All three activities teach children phonics they can actually put immediately into use as they go about all the reading and writing they do during the school day.

chapter 9

Spelling Activities

All the activities described in the previous chapters of this book help children become better spellers. Word-wall activities focus specifically on high-frequency words. On-the-back activities help children learn how to spell words that rhyme with starred word-wall words and word-wall words with endings. Children focus both on spelling and reading words as they engage in Making Words, Rounding Up the Rhymes, and Using Words You Know. Reading/Writing Rhymes activities for rhymes with two common spelling patterns help children begin to notice which rhyming pattern to use and help them learn some common homophones—words like *sail* and *sale,* which are pronounced the same but have different spellings and meanings. Once children have some facility at spelling and decoding based on patterns, they need their attention drawn more directly to spelling patterns. This chapter contains two activities—What Looks Right? and Word Sorting and Hunting—which help children hone their spelling skills.

What Looks Right?

What Looks Right? is an activity by which children learn that good spelling requires visual memory and how to use their visual memory for words along with a dictionary to determine the correct spelling of a word. In English, words that have the same spelling pattern usually rhyme. If you are reading and you come to the unknown words *plight* and *trite,* you can easily figure out their pronunciation by accessing the pronunciation associated with other *ight* or *ite* words you can read and spell. The fact that there are two common spelling patterns with the same pronunciation is not a problem when you are trying to read an unfamiliar-in-print word, but it is a problem when you are trying to spell it. If you were writing and trying to spell *trite* or *plight,* they could as easily be spelled *t-r-i-g-h-t* and *p-l-i-t-e.* The only way to know which is the correct spelling is to write it one way and see if it "looks right" or check your probable spelling in a dictionary. What Looks Right? is an activity to help children learn how to use these two important self-monitoring spelling strategies.

Here is a sample lesson for the *oat–ote* pattern. Using an overhead projector or the board, create two columns and head each with an *oat–ote* word most of your children can both read and spell. Have the children set up two columns on their paper to match your model:

coat   vote

Have the children pronounce and spell the words, and lead them to realize that the words rhyme but have a different spelling pattern. Tell them that there are many words that rhyme with *coat* and *vote* and that you can't tell just by saying the words which spelling patterns they will have. Next say a word that rhymes with *coat* and *vote,* and write it both ways, saying, "If the word is spelled like *coat,* it will be *g-o-a-t.* If it is spelled like *vote,* it will be *g-o-t-e.*" Write these two possible spellings under the appropriate word.

Tell the children to decide which one "looks right" to them and to write only the one they think is correct. As soon as each child decides which one looks right and writes it in the correct column, have each child use the dictionary to see if that spelling can be found. If the children cannot find the one that looked right, then have them look up the other possible spelling. Cross out the spelling you wrote that is not correct and continue with some more examples. For each word, again mention, "If it is spelled like *coat,* it will be *g-o-a-t,* but if it is spelled like *vote,* it will be *g-o-t-e.*" Write the word both ways, and have each child write it the way it looks right and then look in the dictionary to see if the word is spelled the way the child thought.

Here is what your columns of words would look like after several examples:

coat   vote
goat   ~~gote~~
boat   ~~bote~~
float   ~~flote~~
~~noat~~   note
~~quoat~~   quote

throat thr~~oa~~te
bloat bl~~oa~~te

To make your lesson more multileveled, include some longer words in which the last syllable rhymes with *coat* and *vote*. Proceed just as before to write the word both ways and have children choose the one that looks right, write that word, and look for it in the dictionary. For the *coat–vote* lesson, here are three longer words you might use:

pro~~m~~oat promote
de~~v~~oat devote
re~~m~~oat remote

Here is a lesson for the *ait–ate* pattern. Notice that several of these pairs are both words. Children should find both *gate/gait* and *plate/plait*. This is an excellent time to talk about homophones and how the dictionary can help you decide which word to use. Also notice the words written at the bottom. Whenever we think of common words such as *great, eight, weight,* and *straight* that don't follow the pattern, we point these out to children, explaining that most—but not all—words that rhyme with *date* and *wait* are spelled a-t-e or a-i-t.

What Looks Right? is a versatile strategy and can be used to help children become better spellers of longer words. Here are two lessons for the *tion/sion* and *le/el/al* patterns.

While you are working with all these rhyming words is a wonderful time to have your children write some poetry. Select a poem or two your children will like, and read it to them several times. Then have them decide which words rhyme and whether or not the rhyming words have the same spelling patterns. Using these poems as models

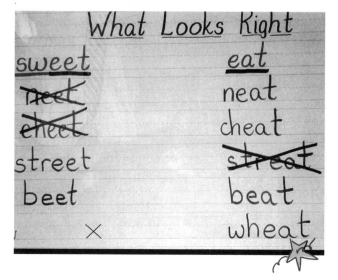

Here is the beginning of a What Looks Right lesson for the *eet–eat* pattern.

and the rhyming words you have collected as part of your spelling pattern lessons, students can write some interesting rhyming poetry.

<u>date</u>	<u>wait</u>
~~date~~	bait
fate	~~fait~~
hate	~~hait~~
skate	~~skait~~
gate	gait
plate	plait
state	~~stait~~
rebate	~~rebait~~
debate	~~debait~~
donate	~~donait~~
hibernate	~~hibernait~~

**straight   eight   weight   great

<u>motion</u>	<u>pension</u>
action	~~acsion~~
station	~~stasion~~
~~mantion~~	mansion
mention	~~mension~~
lotion	~~losion~~
nation	~~nasion~~
~~tention~~	tension
attention	~~attension~~
~~extention~~	extension
~~divition~~	division
multiplication	~~multiplicasion~~
~~television~~	television
vacation	~~vacasion~~
~~collition~~	collision

<u>people</u>	<u>model</u>	<u>animal</u>
~~travle~~	travel	~~traval~~
little	~~littel~~	~~littal~~
~~channle~~	channel	~~channal~~
~~locle~~	~~locel~~	local
~~equle~~	~~equel~~	equal
~~loyle~~	~~loyel~~	loyal
settle	~~settel~~	~~settal~~
poodle	~~poodel~~	~~poodal~~

bubble	bubbel	bubbal
tunnle	tunnel	tunnal
normle	normel	normal
generle	generel	general
possible	possibel	possibal
invisible	invisibel	invisibal
principle	principel	principal

Word Sorting and Hunting

Word Sorts (Henderson, 1990) have long been advocated as an activity to help children know what to attend to, and to develop the habit of analyzing words to look for patterns. There are a variety of ways to do Word Sorts, but the basic principles are always the same. Children look at words and sort them into categories based on spelling patterns and sound. Children say the words and look at how they are spelled. They learn that to go in a certain category, the words must "sound the same and look the same." After sorting words chosen by the teacher, children hunt for other words in books, magazines, and other print around them and then sort these additional words for the patterns as well. In word hunts, teachers help students identify the patterns and then direct children to locate those patterns as they occur naturally in other print sources.

In many classes, different groups of children are working on different levels of sorts. Many teachers do a directed sorting lesson with a group of children first, and then the children continue sorting and hunting in their groups or in partner formats. Here is an example of how one teacher manages several different levels of spellers using a variety of sorting formats.

The teacher is meeting with a group of children who need to work with the various spellings of the vowel *a*. She has divided a transparency into four columns, and the children have all divided their papers into four columns. The teacher heads each column with a vowel pattern and a word the children know that has that pattern. The children set up their columns just like those on the transparency. Question marks are put in the last column to indicate the place to put other words with *a* that don't fit in the first three columns.

a	ai	a-e	???
cat	rain	make	are

As children write each word, the teacher helps them focus on the sound of the *a* and the spelling. *Cat* has just an *a* and the *a* says *a* like in *apple*. *Rain* has an *ai* and is pronounced like *ape*. *Make* is spelled with an *a*, a consonant letter, and an *e*, and the *a* is also pronounced like *ape*. *Are* looks like *make* but does not sound like *make*, so it heads the ??? column. The teacher then shows children words with *a* and has them read each word and decide which column it goes in. To go in a column, it must both look the same and sound the same. The first four words the children see and pronounce are *map, name, paid,* and *pad.* The children pronounce them, stretching out the sound of the vowel, and write them in the appropriate column, and the teacher writes them in the column on the transparency:

a	ai	a-e	???
<u>cat</u>	<u>rain</u>	<u>make</u>	<u>are</u>
map	paid	name	
pad			

The next word is *have.* The children want to immediately write it under *make,* but the teacher has them stretch it out, and they decide that it looks like *make* but sounds like *cat.* It has to go into the ??? column. The teacher continues showing them words containing the letter *a,* which they pronounce and then write in the correct column. They have some trouble with *taste* because there are two consonants between the vowels, but the teacher explains that the pattern is *a* and one or more consonants and the *e,* and they decide it can go with *make.* They decide that *saw* and *park* have to go in the ??? column along with *was.* Here is what their papers and the transparency look like when 15 words have been sorted.

a	ai	a-e	???
<u>cat</u>	<u>rain</u>	<u>make</u>	<u>are</u>
map	paid	name	have
pad	wait	taste	saw
fast	brain	rate	park
jazz		safe	was

On the following day, the children in this group work by themselves. One member of the group is the leader and gets to "play teacher." He shows each word (on index cards prepared by the teacher), has the group pronounce the word, and then writes it on the transparency after the group members have written it on their sheets. If there is disagreement on which column a word should go in, the leader does not write it anywhere but puts it aside to ask the teacher about when the teacher returns to check their work. At the end of this second day, their papers and the transparency look like this:

a	ai	a-e	???
<u>cat</u>	<u>rain</u>	<u>make</u>	<u>are</u>
map	paid	name	have
pad	wait	taste	saw

fast	brain	rate	park
jazz	jail	safe	was
lamp	main	crane	Paul
crash	fail	date	want
brag	bait	case	
pant	drain	place	

Meanwhile, on the second day, while this group is working on its own with a "play teacher," the real teacher is doing a Word Sort introduction with a group of children who are working with spelling changes when *s* is added to words. This group's papers and transparency have these three columns:

s	es	ies
cats	churches	babies

Working with this group, the teacher shows them words, which they pronounce and then write in the appropriate column. At the end of the first day, their columns look like this:

s	es	ies
cats	churches	babies
animals	boxes	ladies
whales	lunches	puppies
crabs	branches	berries
cameras	ashes	parties
cars	taxes	countries

The only word that is difficult for this group is *whales.* Some children think it should go in the "es" column because it ends with *es,* but they decide that what you are focusing on is what was added, and since the word *whale* ends in *e,* only the *s* was added.

On the next day, the group working with *a* works with partners to find more words with *a* for their group to sort on the fourth day. Each set of partners is given 10 index cards and told to find "10 terrific words with *a.*" They write the word they find in big letters on one side of the card, and then, on the other side, they print the key word (in teeny letters) to show what column they think it goes in. Meanwhile, the *s, es, ies* group is doing its "play teacher day," and the real teacher is doing a sort introduction with another group of students who are sorting words with vowels followed by *r* into these columns:

ar	or	er	ir	ur	???
car	for	her	bird	curl	work

After sorting with the teacher today, this group will work in a "play teacher" group on the second day, and then work with partners on the third day to find "10 terrific words" and write them on index cards for their group to sort on the fourth day.

Children in every grade are at all different levels in their spelling abilities. Teachers who are good "kid watchers" look at how children spell words in their first-draft writing to decide what spelling patterns children are ready to learn. The arrangement just described shows how teachers might work with children on a number of different spelling levels. In this classroom, the procedure for each group was:

Day 1. Teacher-directed introduction of a new sort.

Day 2. Group continues to sort words created by teacher under the direction of a "play teacher."

Day 3. Partners work together to find 10 terrific words for their group to sort tomorrow. Teacher checks their cards before their group convenes again.

Day 4. Group convenes and each partnership gets to "play teacher" by presenting its 10 terrific words to the group to be written in the correct columns.

Day 5. Children in group hunt for more words or choose words they really like for each pattern and copy them into a page in their spelling notebook, putting words in the correct columns.

Word sorting and hunting are wonderful activities to develop spelling and decoding skills because children are actively involved in discovering "how words work." Many teachers post charts with the categories the class has worked on, and children are encouraged to add words that fit the pattern any time they find them in anything they are reading. Some children keep word notebooks and add words they find that fit particular categories as they find them throughout the year. In classrooms in which word sorting and hunting are regular activities, children love meeting a "new word" and thinking about where it might fit in all the various categories they have worked on. Most children love collecting things—word sorting and hunting encourage word collecting! The best source for information about word sorting and hunting is *Words Their Way*, 3rd ed. (2004) by Donald Bear, Marcia Invernizzi, Shane Templeton, and Francine Johnston.

Summary: How All the Decoding and Spelling Activities Are Multilevel

All the activities in Part Three have "something for everyone." Regardless of where your students are in their phonics and spelling abilities, there are things they can learn from each lesson format.

Making Words lessons are multilevel in a number of ways. Each lesson begins with short, easy words and progresses to some longer, more complex words. Every Making Words lesson ends by the teacher asking, "Has anyone figured out the word we can make if we use all our letters?" Figuring out the secret word that can be made from all the letters in the limited time available is a challenge to even our most advanced readers. Making Words also includes children with very limited literacy who enjoy manipulating the letters and making the words, even if they don't get them completely made, until the word is made with the big pocket chart letters. By ending each lesson with sorting the words into patterns and then using those patterns to read and spell some new words, we help children of all levels to see how they can use the patterns they see in words to read and spell other words.

While rounding up the rhymes, some children are still developing their phonemic awareness as they decide which words rhyme and learn that rhyming words usually—but not always—have the same spelling pattern. As they use the words rounded up to read and spell new words, children who need it are getting practice with beginning letter substitution. Children who already have well-developed phonemic awareness and beginning letter knowledge are practicing the important strategy of using known words to decode and spell unknown rhyming words.

Using Words You Know lessons provide children who still need it with lots of practice with rhyming words and with the idea that spelling pattern and rhyme are connected. Depending on what they already know, some children realize how words they know can help them decode whereas other children realize how these words help them spell. If you want to make the lesson a bit more multilevel at the upper end, include a few longer words that rhyme and help students see how their known words can help them spell the rhyming part of longer words.

Reading/Writing Rhymes and What Looks Right? are perhaps the most multilevel activities. All beginning letters, including the common single consonants and the less common, more complex digraphs and blends, are reviewed each time the teacher distributes the onset cards for Reading/Writing Rhymes. Phonemic awareness is developed as children say all the rhyming words and blend the vowel pattern with the beginning letters. Children whose word awareness is more sophisticated learn that there are often two spellings for the long vowel patterns and develop their visual checking sense as they see the rhyming words with the different patterns. They also learn the correct spelling for many of the common homophones. The addition of some longer rhyming words helps them learn how to decode and spell longer words. In What Looks Right? children learn to use the dictionary to check a possible spelling. They also learn how the dictionary can help you decide which way to spell a word when there are two words that sound the same but have different spellings and meanings.

Word sorting and hunting are made multilevel by forming groups of children who indicate through their writing that they are ready to focus on particular patterns. The teacher then sets up a schedule so that different groups work with the teacher or together in cooperative formats on different days. The groups are not fixed but rather formed and re-formed as spelling needs and growth are evidenced.

Children are always going to be at different levels in all their abilities. Some run faster than others. Some are better musicians; others are better artists. No matter what we are teaching, we need to stretch our instruction so that there is something for everyone to learn. Multilevel does not mean there is something for every level of reader to learn every minute. It does mean that the activity we are engaging the children in has scope—a variety of things that can be learned depending on what is already known. Multilevel does not imply that everyone learns the same thing—but rather that everyone learns something and feels some sense of success and satisfaction with the activity.

Pick up any newspaper or magazine and read the first few sentences of any article and notice the big words—words that have eight or more letters:

> The SAT—*Scholastic Aptitude* Test—*denounced* as biased and *ineffective* by many *consumers* is still the *gatekeeper* in most *American* schools. College *admissions officers* often *downplay* the *significance* of the exam in the *application* process but then brag about their school's scores in *recruitment brochures.*
>
> *Historically,* as a strike *deadline approaches,* the labor *negotiators go underground* and stop talking to the media. Fear of having the talks *derailed* by leaks causes both sides to stop talking and keep *bargaining.*

The first thing that strikes you in looking at these big words is that these big words are the "meaning-carrying" words. Without them, you wouldn't know very much. The second thing you should notice is that these words are relatively low-frequency words. You could read many articles and pages in books before once again encountering *recruitment, historically,* and *derailed.*

Starting at about the fourth-grade level, most of what we read contains a high percentage of big, relatively unfamiliar, low-frequency words. Because these big words contain most of the meaning, we cannot comprehend what we read unless we can pronounce and access meaning for these words. All good readers are able to quickly pronounce and associate meaning with words they have rarely ever read before. How does this happen? How did you pronounce and make meaning for words such as *admissions, derailed,* and *underground* the first time you encountered them in your reading?

Linguists, who study how language words, tell us that in English, morphemes are the keys to unlocking the pronunciation, spelling, and meaning for big words. Morphemes are roots, prefixes, and suffixes that combine in a variety of ways to make up big words. The word *admission* is simply the word *admit*—with the spelling changes that always occur when *sion* is added to words ending in *t.* The first time you saw *admissions,* your brain probably accessed similar words such as *permission, omission,* and *emission.* Using these other similar words, you quickly pronounced *admission.* Since you were probably aware that when you *permit* something, you give your *permission,* when you *omit* something, you have an *omission,* and the fumes that your car *emits* are called *emissions,* you probably also recognized the relationship between the word you had read many times—*admit*—and this new word *admissions.* Similarly, pronouncing and making meaning for *derailed* was not difficult if your brain thought of similar words such as *deported* and *declassified. Underground* is a compound word—its pronunciation and meaning are obvious by thinking of the pronunciation and meaning of the two root words, *under* and *ground.*

Morphemes—roots, prefixes, and suffixes—are the keys to unlocking the pronunciation, spelling, and meaning for big words. When you see a big new word you have never encountered before in your reading, your brain thinks of similar big words and uses these big words and the understanding it has about how these big words work to quickly pronounce and access meaning for the new big word. But what if your brain doesn't have very many big words stored there? What if you have some big words but you have never realized how they were related to your smaller words? Children who lack big words that they can quickly access, and associate meaning for, are helpless from fourth grade up when they encounter big words.

When describing how children decode short words, we emphasized the importance of patterns. The patterns in short words are the onsets and rimes. When good readers encounter an unfamiliar short word in their reading, they look at the beginning letters—the onset—and assign it a pronunciation. Next, they look at the rime—the vowel and what follows—and assign it a pronunciation. They blend these two parts together to produce a reasonable pronunciation for the word. When a good speller needs to spell a new word, he or she thinks of other words that rhyme. If there are two possible spelling patterns for the rhyme, the good speller writes the word and then does a visual check to see if it "looks right." If not, the other spelling is tried and, if still unsure and the correct spelling is important, the dictionary is consulted. Good readers decode and spell new words by comparing them to words they can already can read and spell.

Decoding and spelling big words—multisyllabic words with anywhere from 8 to 20 letters—is also dependent on patterns from similar words. The chapters in Part Four will help children build a store of big words and help them learn to use their big words to decode, spell, and build meaning for unfamiliar big words.

Decoding and Spelling Big Words

In this chapter, you will find ways to help your students build their store of big words and learn how to use those big words to spell and decode other big words.

Big-Word Collectors

Kids love to collect things—sports cards, butterflies, shells, autographs. Teachers who want their students to be big-word experts can motivate their students by encouraging them to become big-word collectors! The collections can be both individual and classroom projects. Some collections can be permanent collections—needed for all kinds of reading and writing. Other collections can come and go as new topics, themes, and units are explored. Here are some of the ways teachers encourage big-word collecting.

Topic Word Boards

Reserve one of the bulletin boards in your room for use as a topic word board. Display some pictures related to the unit and tell students you need them to help you find big words needed to learn about the topic. Leave a supply of colored index cards next to the board, and as you and your students explore the unit, ask them for suggestions of topic-related words to add to the collection. When students suggest words, have them explain why that word is particularly important to the topic. Write words the class agrees belong in that collection with a black, thick permanent marker. Add words gradually and make sure the class agrees they are needed. Students who have input into the selection of the words to be learned have ownership and begin to see these words as "their words," not just "more words to learn."

As you and the students explore the topic, call attention occasionally to a word when it is used in discussion, reading, or other learning experiences. Help students to focus on the spelling of the words by having them chant the spelling (cheerleader style) with you. Then have them close their eyes and chant the spelling again. When you have a few minutes, challenge them to write a sentence that uses as many of the words as they can and still makes a sensible sentence. As students write about what they are learning, encourage them to use the words and to refer to the board for correct spellings. Help students to develop positive attitudes toward learning big words by pointing out that every field has some critical words, the use of which separates the pros from the amateurs.

Add another chart after a few weeks and let children suggest words that should be added to both. In addition to collecting big words to replace "tired, overworked" words, this chart strategy also works well for having students be on the lookout and collect specific kinds of words such as compound words. Keep charts displayed as long as you can, given your limited classroom space, and then use the procedure described for topic boards to get meanings, examples, sentences, and visuals written on the back of each card and the cards filed according to category in some accessible way.

When the unit is over and you begin another topic on this board, have different students write a personal meaning, an example sentence, and draw some kind of visual on the back of each card. Alphabetize these cards and place them in your collection. A file box arranged according to topic takes little space and is easily accessible by all. As the year goes on, your collection will grow to an impressive number. Encourage students to find a word in this box if they remember having used the word and need to find it later in the year. Take time occasionally to let students count words and use words across topics in a variety of word-sorting and categorizing activities. We all love looking at our collections from time to time, marveling at how they are growing and comparing old items with newly acquired ones.

Collect Big Words Needed for
All Kinds of Reading and Writing

Another way to help students begin to notice and appreciate the power of words is to have them on the lookout for big words that "say it better." Focus on a word that you are tired of seeing in their writing and begin a chart for them to help you collect "Big Words for *Said*." Add a few that students suggest immediately and then add more gradually as students encounter them in their reading or discussions. For each word, have students give examples of sentences in which the word they want added would be a better word, and have the class as a whole decide if it is worth adding to the chart.

Big Words for Said

answered	confessed	promised
whispered	murmured	reminded
suggested	explained	muttered
stammered	exclaimed	pleaded
snickered	bragged	stuttered
requested		

Big Words Describing People

unhappy	curious	tremendous
delighted	famished	nervous
thrilled	patient	brilliant
overjoyed	miserable	mysterious
frightened	lovable	hilarious
paralyzed	astonished	

Compound Words

anybody	basketball	motorcycle	watermelon	downstairs	strawberry
jellyfish	everyone	woodpecker	applesauce	homework	football
birthday	keyboard	grandmother	toothbrush	rattlesnake	doorbell
boyfriend	headset	grasshopper	playground	starfish	rollerblade

Personal Collections

Once your students begin to understand the power of big words and how much fun it is to collect them, encourage them to start their own collections. Some teachers have students bring large, tabbed notebooks and label the different sections for topics of particular interest to each student. Other teachers provide small file boxes for each child, with dividers and 3 × 5 index cards. Children should establish categories they are interested in—baseball, computers, sea animals, Mexico, Disneyworld, scuba diving. As students find big words related to their categories, they write these on one side of the card and complete the card with a personal meaning, sentence example, and visual on the back, just as they do for the cards created for the class collections. (Children who don't like to draw love to find appropriate visuals on the Web or in your clip-art collection! Encourage them to cut and paste.)

Once your students have begun their own big-word collections, give them time every few weeks to share the new words they have found and why these words are important to their topics. You may want to form small collecting groups, particularly if you have children with similar categories. Provide extra cards so that they can make extras to trade with their like-minded friends.

A wide vocabulary is one of the clearest indicators of intelligence, education, and literacy. Children who collect big words related to topics of interest to them increase their vocabularies in that area, and many of the words have meanings that carry over to other topics. Perhaps most important, their attitude toward big words changes. Instead of looking away and "skipping over" big new words, your students will approach big words with an "I wonder what it is. Maybe I need it" attitude that makes all the difference. Children who can read and spell some big words have the patterns to decode and spell lots of others. Regardless of the topic, children with personal big-word collections acquire facility and confidence with big words.

Here are some of the words one boy had in his basketball word collection. Notice how many of these words have application beyond the world of basketball and how many words have patterns applicable to other words.

technical	offensive	defensive	tournament	turnover	rebounds
coliseum	underdogs	referee	victorious	undefeated	semifinals
challenge	teammates	possession	contention	physical	dominate

Modeling: How to Figure Out a Big Word

When you model, you show someone how to do something. In real life, we use modeling constantly to teach skills. We would not think of explaining how to ride a bike. Rather, we demonstrate and talk about what we are doing as the learner watches what we do and listens to our explanation. Vocabulary introduction is a good place to model for students how you figure out the pronunciation of a word. The word should be shown in a sentence context so that students are reminded that words must have the right letters in the right places and make sense. Following is an example of how you might model for students one way to decode *entertainment:*

> "I am going to write a sentence on the board that has a big word in it. I will 'think aloud' how I might figure out this one. After I show you how I decode this one, I will let several of you model how you would decode other words."

Write on the board: *Different people like different kinds of entertainment.*

> "Now I am going to read up to the big word and tell you how I might figure it out. If you figure out the word before I do, please don't say it and ruin my performance!"

Read the sentence and stop when you get to *entertainment.*

> "This is a long word, but I can probably figure it out if I think of some other words I know."

Cover all but *enter.*

> "The first chunk is a word I know—*enter.* The second chunk is like *container* and *maintain.*"

Write *container* and *maintain* on the board, underlining the *tain.*

> "Finally, I know the last chunk is like *argument* and *moment.*"

Write *argument* and *moment* on the board, underlining the *ment.*

> "Now I will put the chunks together: *enter-tain-ment.* Yes, that's a word I know, and it makes sense in the sentence because my brother and I certainly are different and we don't like the same TV shows or movies or anything."

Since English is not a language in which letters or chunks have only one sound, you might also write the word *mountain* on the board, underlining the *tain* and pointing out to students that the letters *t-a-i-n* also commonly have the sound you hear at the end of *mountain*. Have students try pronouncing *entertainment* with the different sounds for the *tain* chunk. Point out that it sounds right and makes a word you know when you use the sound of *tain* you know from *maintain* and *container*. Remind students that if they use the probable sound of letters together with the sense of what they are reading, they can figure out many more words than if they just pay attention to the letter sounds, ignoring what makes sense, or if they just guess something that makes sense, ignoring the letter sounds.

For *entertainment,* the chunks only helped with the pronunciation of the word. Sometimes the word has morphemes—prefixes, suffixes, or root words—that also help with the meaning of the word. The next example shows what a teacher might do and say to introduce the word *international*.

Write on the board or overhead transparency: *The thinning of the ozone layer is an international problem.*

> "Today, we are going to look at a big word that is really just a little word with a prefix added to the beginning and a suffix added to the end."

Underline *nation.*

> "Who can tell me this word? Yes, that's the word *nation,* and we know *nation* is another word for *country.* Now let's look at the prefix that comes before *nation.*"

Underline *inter.*

> "This prefix is *inter.* You probably know *inter* from words like *interrupt* and *internal.* Now let's look at what follows *inter* and *nation.*"

Underline *al.*

> "You know *al* from many words, such as *unusual* and *critical.*"

Write *unusual* and *critical* and underline the *al.*

> "Listen as I pronounce this part of the word."

Underline and pronounce *national.*

> "Notice how the pronunciation of *nation* changes when we put *a-l* on it. Now let's put all the parts together and pronounce the word *inter nation al.*" Let's read the sentence and make sure *international* makes sense."

Have the sentence read and confirm that ozone thinning is indeed a problem for many nations to solve.

> "You can figure out the pronunciation of many big words if you look for common prefixes, such as *inter,* common root words, such as *nation,* and common suffixes, such as *al.*

> "In addition to helping you figure out the pronunciation of a word, prefixes and suffixes sometimes help you know what the word means or where in a sentence we can use the word. The word *nation* names a thing. When we describe a nation, we add the suffix *al* and have *national.* The prefix *inter* often means "between or among." Something that is *international* is between many nations. The Olympics are the best example of an *international* sports event."

This sample lesson for introducing the word *international* demonstrates how a teacher can help students see and use morphemes to decode polysyllabic words. As in the sample lesson for *entertainment,* the teacher points out words students might know that have the same chunks—in this case, morphemes. In addition, meaning clues yielded by the morphemes are provided whenever appropriate.

Word Detectives

There are two questions I would like to put into the mouths of every teacher of children from fourth grade through high school. These two questions are:

> "Do I know any other words that look and sound like this word?"

> "Are any of these look-alike/sound-alike words related to each other?"

The answer to the first question should help students with pronouncing and spelling the word. The answer to the second question should help students discover what, if any, meaning relationships exist between this new word and others in their meaning vocabulary stores. This guideline and these two simple questions could be used by any teacher of any subject area. Imagine that students in a mathematics class encounter the new word:

> *equation*

The teacher demonstrates and gives examples of equations and helps build meaning for the concept. Finally, the teacher asks the students to pronounce *equation* and see if they know any other words that look and sound like *equation.* Students think of:

addition	multiplication	nation	vacation
equal	equator		

The teacher lists the words, underlining the parts that look the same. Students pronounce the words, emphasizing the part that is pronounced the same. The teacher then points out to the students that thinking of a word that looks and sounds the same as a new word will help you quickly remember how to pronounce the new word and will also help you spell the new word.

Next the teacher explains that words, like people, sometimes look and sound alike but are not related. If this is the first time this analogy is used, the teacher will want to spend some time talking with the students about people with red hair, green eyes, and so on who have some parts that look alike but are not related and others who are.

> "Not all people who look alike are related, but some are. This is how words work too. Words are related if there is something about their meaning that is the same. After we find look-alike, sound-alike words that will help us spell and pronounce new words, we try to think of any ways these words might be in the same meaning family."

With help from the teacher, the children discover that *equal, equator,* and *equation* are related because the meaning of *equal* is in all three. An equation has to have equal quantities on both sides of the equal signs. The equator is an imaginary line that divides the earth into two equal halves.

Imagine that the students who were introduced to equations on Monday during math and were asked to think of look-alike, sound-alike words and consider if any of these words might be "kinfolks" had a science lesson on Tuesday in which they did some experiments with the students using *thermometers* and *barometers.* At the close of the lesson, the teacher pointed to these words and helped them notice that the *meters* chunk was pronounced and spelled the same and asked the students if they thought these words were just look-alikes or were related to one another. The students would probably conclude that you used them both to measure things and the *meters* chunk must be related to measuring, like in *kilometers.* When asked to think of look-alike, sound-alike words for the first chunk, students thought of *baron* for *barometers* but decided these two words were probably not related. For *thermometer,* they thought of *thermal* and *thermostat* and decided that all these words had to do with heat or temperature and were related.

Now imagine that this lucky class of students had a social studies lesson on Wednesday during which the teacher pointed out the new word *international* and asked the two critical questions, a music lesson on Thursday in which they were preparing for a trip to the *symphony,* and a tennis lesson on Friday in which they practiced their *forehand* and *backhand* strokes and the teacher asked the two critical questions about these crucial tennis words.

Throughout their school day, children encounter many new words. Because English is such a morphologically related language, most new words can be connected to other words by their spelling and pronunciation, and many new words have meaning-related words already known to the student. Some clever, word-sensitive children become word detectives on their own. They notice the patterns and use these to learn and retrieve words. Others, however, try to learn to pronounce, spell, and associate meaning with each of these words as separate, distinct entities. This is a difficult task that becomes almost impossible as students move through the grades and the number of new words increases each year. Readers do not need to be taught every possible pattern because the brain is programmed to look for patterns. Some students, however, do not know what the important patterns in words are and that these patterns can help you with pronouncing, spelling, and meanings for words. Asking the two critical questions for key vocabulary introduced in any content area would add only a few minutes to the introduction of key content vocabulary and would turn many students into word detectives.

 # The Wheel

The popular game show *Wheel of Fortune* is premised on the idea that meaning and some letters allow you to figure out many words. In this game, meaning is provided by the category to which the words belong. A variation of this game can be used to introduce polysyllabic words and teach students to use meaning and all the letters they know. Here is how to play The Wheel.

Remind students that many words can be figured out, even when we can't decode all the chunks, if we think about what makes sense and whether it has the parts we do know in the right places. Ask students who have watched *Wheel of Fortune* to explain how it is played. Then explain, step by step, how your version of The Wheel will be different:

1. Contestants guess all letters without considering if they are consonants or vowels.
2. They must have all letters filled in before they can say the word. (This is to encourage them to learn to spell.)
3. They will win paper clips instead of great prizes.
4. Vanna will not be there to turn letters!

Write the category for the game on the board and draw blanks for each letter in the first word.

Have a student begin by asking,

"Is there a . . . ?"

If the student guesses a correct letter, fill that letter in. Give that student one paper clip for each time that letter occurs. Let the student continue to guess letters until he or she gets a "No." When a student asks for a letter that is not there, write the letter above the puzzle and go on to the next student.

Make sure that all letters are filled in before anyone is allowed to guess. (This really shows them the importance of spelling and attending to common spelling patterns.)

Give the person who correctly guesses the word five bonus paper clips. Just as in other games, if someone says the answer out of turn, immediately award the bonus paper clips to the person whose turn it was. The student having the most paper clips at the end is the winner. Here is an example:

Teacher draws nine blanks on the board and says, "The category is sports. Our first word has nine letters. Al, guess a letter."

_ _ _ _ _ _ _ _ _

Al asks for a *t*. There is no *t*, so the teacher moves on to David who asks for an *r*. There is no *r* either. Nor is there an *o*, which Carol asks for. But Jon asks for and gets an *a*.

_ _ _ _ _ _ a _

Jon goes again and asks for an *s*.

s _ _ _ _ _ a _

Next, he asks for an *e*.

s e _ _ _ _ _ a _

Next, he asks for a *d*. There is no *d*, so the turn passes to Paula, who asks for an *n*.

s e _ _ _ _ n a _

Next, Paula asks for an *m*.

s e m _ _ _ n a _

Then she asks for an *i*.

s e m i _ i n a _

The light dawns in Paula's eyes. She quickly asks for an *f* and *l* and wins by correctly spelling and pronouncing *semifinal*!

 # Mystery Word Match

Mystery Word Match is a game I developed to help children learn to look for familiar chunks in unfamiliar big words. To begin the game, the teacher has a polysyllabic word in mind. This big word is the "mystery word." The teacher first draws the number of short blanks to indicate the number of letters in the mystery word. He then writes three clue words under these letter blanks or spaces.

Each clue word has a chunk of the mystery word in the same position in the word and with the same pronunciation. Sometimes the chunks are syllables and sometimes they are larger than syllables. It is important that students not only focus on the syllables because, when they are decoding a big word, they access from their word store the words with the largest chunks. For the word *entertainment,* for example, students might have recognized three chunks—*enter, tain,* and *ment.* Sometimes the chunks are roots, prefixes, and suffixes, but sometimes they are just familiar parts.

As each clue word is written, the teacher and students pronounce it and put it in a meaningful sentence. Before guessing which part of which clue word is in the mystery word, the students should pronounce the words again to assure that everyone can easily pronounce the clue words.

Here is an example of how a round of Mystery Word Match would be played.

The teacher draws eight short lines on the board and says, "Our mystery word has eight letters." The teacher then writes the three clue words under the lines. The students and teacher pronounce each and put each in a sentence. Before beginning play, all three clue words are once more pronounced by everybody.

_ _ _ _ _ _ _ _

testimony
celebrate
direction

A student is chosen and begins by asking if the mystery word begins, has a middle like, or ends like one of the clues. If the answer is "yes," the teacher writes these letters on the correct lines and the student continues to ask. If the answer is "no," the turn goes to the next student.

> *Carl:*   "Does the mystery word begin like *direction*?"
>
> *Teacher:*   "No, I am sorry. It is Terry's turn."
>
> *Terry:*   "Does the mystery word end like *direction*?"
>
> *Teacher:*   "No, I am sorry. It is Jared's turn."
>
> *Jared:*   "Does the mystery word have a middle like *direction*?"
>
> *Teacher:*   "Yes, it does."

Teacher writes *re* on the appropriate letter lines:

_ _ r e _ _ _ _

> *Teacher:*   "Jared, you may ask another question."
>
> *Jared:*   "Does the mystery word begin like *celebrate*?"
>
> *Teacher:*   "Yes, it does."

Technology Tip

Mystery Word Match was in the early editions of *Phonics They Use*. I dropped it out of the third edition, however, because it was so hard for teachers to make up good clue words. The first chunk was easy—you could simply look in the dictionary. But the middle and end chunks were much harder. Before a book is revised, it goes out to reviewers who make suggestions. One of the reviewers bemoaned "the mysterious disappearance of Mystery Word Match." I wished I had a way to tell him or her that I gave up on it because teachers needed to be able use mystery words that fit their curriculum and it was just too hard to do. Then I thought about the Internet. Surely, there was a site that would match parts of words. I put my husband (who is much better at searching the Web than I) to work, and, in no time at all, he had found several sites. The one I use is www.onelook.com. You put asterisks around the letters you are looking to match and instantly get lots of matches. (Be sure the match has the same pronunciation.) A special thanks to the reviewer whose comment is responsible for the return of this fun and educational big-word game!

Teacher writes *ce* on appropriate lines:

<u>c</u> <u>e</u> <u>r</u> <u>e</u> _ _ _ _

Teacher: "Jared, you may ask another question."

Jared: "Does the mystery word end like *testimony*?"

Teacher writes *mony*.

<u>c</u> <u>e</u> <u>r</u> <u>e</u> <u>m</u> <u>o</u> <u>n</u> <u>y</u>

Jared pronounces the word, *ceremony*, and wins this round of Mystery Word Match.

Mystery Word Match is a simple game but students of all ages love playing it. A few cautions, however. The child who finishes putting the word in the letter blanks must also pronounce the word. If she cannot, play passes to the next person. If you will enforce this rule and if you will have the clue words pronounced several times before beginning, even your struggling readers will pay attention to the pronunciation of the parts of the clue words. Another issue is students who "call out the answer" when it is not their turn. If that happens, the student whose turn it was is immediately declared the winner and awarded the points. Many teachers have the mystery word worth 10 points to begin with and subtract 1 point for every "no." Under these rules, Jared would have won 8 points for figuring out and pronouncing the mystery word.

You need to use the big words that are part of your curriculum for Mystery Word Match games, but here are some to get you started.

General Vocabulary

mysterious	*expectation*	*destination*
bacterial	respectable	dessert
mystified	limitation	assassination
continuous	explorer	article

transportation	*resolution*	*argument*
reporter	recipe	regulate
transferred	pollution	statement
mutation	insolent	artistic

resistance	*conversation*	*contestant*
insisting	conference	constitution
reformer	overthrow	informant
inheritance	sensation	pretested

Math Vocabulary

multiplication	*geometry*	*perpendicular*
amplify	geography	circular
multimedia	chemistry	expenditures
dedication	thermometer	perfection

denominator	*numerator*	*circumference*
terminator	nucleus	interference
monogram	alligator	incumbent
democracy	commercial	circuitry

equivalent	*equilateral*	*intersection*
turbulent	equivalent	consecutive
cavalry	funeral	international
equitable	gelatin	position

Science Vocabulary

experiment	*microorganism*	*photosynthesis*
nonperishable	microphone	hypothesis
extravagant	disorganized	idiosyncrasy
management	terrorism	photographer

metamorphic	*sedimentary*	*atmosphere*
humorless	secluded	thermostat
metabolic	elementary	attention
geographic	editor	hemisphere

constellation	*precipitation*	*conservation*
interstellar	recipient	consistently
creation	confrontation	casserole
concentrate	prefabricated	innovation

Social Studies Vocabulary

independence	*democracy*	*exploration*
undependable	demolition	deplorable
innocent	literacy	invitation
audience	sacrament	extension

revolution	*constitution*	*communities*
advocate	container	immunize
solution	substituted	compassion
rebellious	attention	activities

population	*republican*	*continent*
accumulated	pelican	constitution
intention	reevaluate	permanent
popularity	unpublished	testify

 Summary

Big words—words of eight or more letters—are the words that carry the meaning of whatever we are reading. There are thousands of them and we don't see any of them very frequently. In order to be a good reader from third grade on, children must have strategies for decoding and spelling big words. Big words are decoded and spelled based on similar patterns from other big words. Many children, however, do not have a store of big words they can fluently read and spell. This chapter has suggested ways of adding big words to the word stores of all the children we teach. In addition, suggestions were made for having children use big words to decode and spell other big words. We used the term *chunk* rather than *syllable* because good readers use the "largest recognizable unit" as they decode and spell unfamiliar words.

Many big words have recognizable roots, prefixes, and suffixes. These morphemic "chunks" are particularly useful because not only do they give clues to pronunciation and spelling, but they also help us determine the meaning of unfamiliar big words. The following chapter will focus specifically on helping children use roots, prefixes, and suffixes to decode, spell, and build meaning for polysyllabic words.

chapter 11

Roots, Prefixes, and Suffixes

Morphemes are meaningful parts of words. The word *internationalize* has four morphemes:

inter—a prefix meaning "between"
nation—a root word
al—a suffix that commonly turns a noun into an adjective
ize—a suffix that commonly turns nouns and adjectives into verbs

Children need to realize that many of the big words they encounter while reading are just words they already know with parts added to the beginning (prefixes) and parts added to the end (suffixes). It is important to note here that it is not the terminology—the jargon—that children need to learn. When you first saw the word *modernize*, your brain didn't say,

"I see the root word *modern* with the prefix *ize.*"

Rather, your brain recognized the familiar parts, put the parts together, and pronounced the word. You may also have used other *ize* known words such as *legalize* and *unionize* to build meaning for *modernize.* This chapter will help children learn how roots, prefixes, and suffixes help them decode, spell, and build meaning for thousands of big words. The focus of this chapter, as of all the other chapters in *Phonics They Use,* is on how to help students use these morphemic parts, not just recognize them.

Teaching Common Prefixes and Suffixes

Four prefixes, *un, re, in* (and *im, ir, il* meaning "not"), and *dis,* account for 58 percent of all prefixed words. Add 16 more prefixes—*en/em, non, in/im* (meaning "in"), *over, mis, sub, pre, inter, fore, de, trans, super, semi, anti, mid,* and *under*—and you can account for 97 percent of all prefixed words (White, Sowell, & Yanagihara, 1989). Children who can read, spell, and attach meaning to these 20 prefixes have a jump start on decoding, spelling, and meaning for a huge number of multisyllabic words.

For suffixes, *s/es, ed,* and *ing* account for 65 percent of the suffixed words. Add *ly, er/or, ion/tion, ible/able, al, y, ness, ity,* and *ment* and you account for 87 percent of the words. The remaining suffixes with some utility are *er/est* (comparative), *ic, ous, en, ive, ful,* and *less* (White, Sowell, & Yanagihara, 1989). Again, learning to read, spell, and understand how meaning is affected for a relatively small number of suffixes gives readers a huge advantage with multisyllabic words.

A Prefix Lesson Framework

The modeling during vocabulary introduction and Word Detectives activities described previously take advantage of whatever words occur in the course of content-area instruction. Most students can also profit from some explicit instruction with the most common prefixes. We teach all the prefixes using the same structure. We begin with words containing the prefixes students already can read and spell and have meaning for. We use these known words to establish the pattern and then move to less familiar words. We include examples of words in which the prefix has a discernible meaning and others in which the prefix helps with pronunciation and spelling but not with meaning. Here is an example lesson that could be used to sensitize students to the prefix *re.*

Write nine words that begin with *re* on index cards. Include three words in which *re* means "back," three words in which *re* means "again," and three words in which *re* is just the first syllable and has no apparent meaning. Use words for which your students are apt to have meanings. Place these words randomly along the chalk ledge, have them pronounced, and ask students what "chunk" the words all have in common. Once students notice that they all begin with *r-e,* arrange the words in three columns on the board and tell the students to think about why you have put together *rebound, return,* and *replace* in one column; *redo, replay,* and *rework* in the second column; and *record, refuse,* and *reveal* in the third column. If students need help, tell them that for one column of *re* words, you can put the word *again* in place of the *re* and still have the meaning of the word. Explain that for another column, you can put the word *back* in place of *re.* Once students have figured out in which column the *re* means "back" and in which *re* means "again," label these columns *back* and *again.* Help students see that when you refuse something, you don't fuse it back or fuse it again. Do the same with *record* and *reveal.*

Back	Again	
rebound	redo	record
return	replay	refuse
replace	rework	reveal

Have students set up their own papers in three columns, the first two headed by *back* and *again* and the last not headed, and have them write the words written on the board. Then say some other *re* words and have students write them in the column they think they belong in. As each word is written, ask someone where they wrote it and how they spelled it. Write it in the appropriate column on the board. Conclude the activity by having all the *re* words read and replacing the *re* with *back* or *again* when appropriate. Help students summarize that sometimes *re* means "back," sometimes *re* means "again," and sometimes *re* is just the first chunk of the word. Some additional words you might use are:

reusable	retire	retreat	rewind
recall	respond	remote	responsible
recoil	rewrite	refund	relief

Once this activity is completed, leave the chart with these *re* words displayed and ask students to hunt for *re* words in their reading for the next several days. When they find a word that begins with *re,* they should decide which category it fits and add it to the chart. At the end of several days, review the chart and help students summarize what they learned about *re* as a pronunciation, spelling, and sometimes meaning chunk in words.

As you do other lessons with prefixes, your message to students should be the same. Prefixes are chunks at the front of words that have predictable pronunciations and spellings. Look for them and depend on them to help you spell and pronounce new words. Sometimes, they also give you meaning clues. If you are unsure about the meaning of a word, see if a common meaning for the prefix can help. Check the meaning you figure out to make sure it makes sense in the context in which you are reading. Here are the most common prefixes, their most common meanings, and examples of words in which the prefix is a meaning help along with examples of words in which the prefix is only a help for spelling and pronouncing the word.

Prefix	Meaning	Meaning Chunk	Spelling/Pronunciation Chunk
re	back	replacement	refrigerator
re	again	rearrange	reward
un	opposite	unfriendly	uncle
in (im, ir, il)	opposite	independent	incident
		impossible	imagine
		irresponsible	irritate
		illegal	illustrate
in (im)	in	invasion	instant
		impression	immense
dis	opposite	dishonest	distress
non	opposite	nonliving	—
en	in	encourage	entire
mis	bad, wrong	misunderstand	miscellaneous
pre	before	prehistoric	present
inter	between	international	interesting
de	opposite/take away	deodorize	delight
sub	under	submarine	subsist
fore	before/in front of	forehead	—
trans	across	transportation	—
super	really big	supermarkets	superintendent
semi	half	semifinal	seminar
mid	middle	midnight	midget
over	too much	overpower	—
under	below	underweight	understand
anti	against	antifreeze	—

The "Unpeelable" Prefixes

In addition to the prefixes, which can be understood by taking them off the root word and then combining the meanings, there are other common prefixes that do not leave recognizable words when they are "peeled off." The prefixes *con/com*, *ex*, *em*, and *per* do add meanings to words, but you have to have a rather advanced understanding of Latin and Greek roots to see the meaning relationships. It is probably best just to help students see how these are predictable spelling and pronunciation chunks rather than try to show students how to analyze these words for meaning clues. Here are some examples for these "unpeelable" prefixes:

Unpeelable Prefix	Examples
com/con	communities, competition, communism
	composer, computer, compassion
	continuous, construction, conclusion
	conversation, constitution, concrete
em	employee, embassy, embryo
ex	expensive, excitement, explain
per	performance, permanent, personality

A Suffix Lesson Framework

Suffixes, like prefixes, are predictable indicators of pronunciation and sometimes signal a meaning relationship. The meaning signaled by suffixes, however, is not usually a meaning change, but rather a change in how and in what position the word can be used in the sentence. *Compose* is what you do. The *composer* is the person doing it. A *composition* is what you have once you have composed. Students need to become aware of how words change when they are signaling different relationships. They also need to realize that there are slight pronunciation changes in root words when suffixes are added.

The first suffixes we teach should be the most familiar to students and have the highest utility. The suffixes *er* and *ion* make particularly useful first lessons.

To teach *er,* write words on index cards that demonstrate the someone or something who does something, some comparative meanings, and some words that just end in *er*. Place the words randomly along the chalk ledge and have students notice that the words all end in *er*. Next, arrange the words in four columns, and help students see that column-one words are all people who do something, column-two words are things that do something, column-three words mean "more," and column-four words are those in which *er* is just the last chunk:

People Who Do	Things That Do	More	
reporter	computer	fatter	cover
photographer	pointer	skinnier	never
teacher	heater	greater	master

Label the first three columns *People Who Do, Things That Do,* and *More.* Do not label the last column. Have pupils set up papers in four columns, labeling and listing the words just as you have done on the board. Call out some *er* words and have students write them in the column they think they belong in. Then have students spell each word and tell you which column to put the word in. Remind students of spelling rules—changing *y* to *i*, doubling letters—as needed. Some *er* words you might use are:

after	richer	fighter	winner
winter	under	heavier	air conditioner
murderer	manager	copier	dishwasher
runner	diaper	writer	typewriter

A common suffix that is always pronounced the same way and that sometimes signals a change from doing to the thing done is *ion*. Students make this shift easily in their speech and need to recognize that the same shift occurs in reading and writing. Write *tion* words on index cards, some of which have a related "doing" word and some of which don't. After students notice that the words all end in *tion* and that the *tion* chunk is pronounced the same, divide the words to form two columns on the board. For example:

collection	nation
election	fraction
attraction	condition

Help students see that when you collect coins, you have a coin *collection;* we elect leaders during an *election;* and you have an *attraction* for someone you are attracted to. In *nation, fraction*, and *condition*, the *tion* is pronounced the same but the meaning of the word is not obvious by looking at the root word. Have students set up their papers in the usual way, then call out words for students to decide which group they fit with. Be sure to have students spell words as you write them on the board and talk about the meaning relationships where appropriate. Here are some starters:

traction	subtraction	construction	rejection
auction	expedition	tradition	interruption
mention	action	pollution	correction

Here are some *sion* words you could use in a similar activity:

confusion	invasion	vision	provision
extension	suspension	passion	expression
collision	mission	tension	explosion

Just as with prefixes, we keep the chart displayed for several days and ask students to add words they find in their reading to the appropriate columns. Here are the most common endings and suffixes, along with example words familiar to most children.

Suffix/Ending	Examples
s/es	heroes, musicians, signatures
(y-i)	communities, discoveries, countries
ed/ing	unfinished, performed, misunderstanding
(drop e)	nonliving, replaced, continuing
(double consonant)	swimming, forgetting
er/est	richest, craziest, bigger
en	forgotten, hidden, chosen
less	hopeless, careless, penniless
ful	beautiful, successful, pitiful
able	valuable, portable, incurable
ible	irresponsible, reversible, horrible
tion	transportation, imagination, solution
sion	invasion, impression, permission
ly	unfriendly, hopelessly, happily
er	composer, reporter, robber
or	governor, dictator, juror
ee	employee, referee, trainee
ian	musician, magician, beautician
ance	performance, attendance, ignorance
ence	independence, conference, persistence
ment	encouragement, punishment, involvement
ness	happiness, goodness, business
y	discovery, jealousy, pregnancy
ity	electricity, popularity, possibility
ant	unpleasant, tolerant, dominant
ent	different, confident, excellent
al	international, political, racial
ive	expensive, inconclusive, competitive
ous	continuous, humorous, ambitious
ic	prehistoric, scenic, specific
ify	classify, beautify, identify
ize	deodorize, modernize, standardize
ture	signature, creature, fracture

Teaching Common Root Words

So far, we have talked about working from prefixes and suffixes back to the root word. Some children find it exciting to see how many different words they can read and understand from just one root word. Students need to learn that the pronunciation of a root word often changes slightly as prefixes and suffixes are added. They also need to learn that the root sometimes helps them to come up with meanings. Some sample root-word activities are described next.

Lessons with Simple Roots

For the first lessons, use some words that students know well to make the point that words they know are often the keys to unlocking the pronunciation, spelling, and meaning for hundreds of other words. *Play* makes a great first lesson.

Write the word *play* on the board. Tell students that a little word like *play* can become a big word when parts are added to the beginning and ending of the word. Write words that have *play* in them. Have the words pronounced and talk about how the meaning of the word changes. Have students suggest other words with *play*. Here are some starters:

plays	played	playing	player	players
playful	playfully	playable	replay	playfulness
misplay	ballplayer	outplay	overplay	playground
playhouse	playoff	playpen	playwright	screenplay

Other roots that have many words include *work*, *agree*, and *create*:

workable	homework	network	rework
working	legwork	housework	outwork
workers	unworkable	nonworker	woodwork
teamwork	overworked	paperwork	schoolwork
workshop	workout	groundwork	hardworking
agree	agreeable	agreeably	disagreement
agreed	agreement	nonagreement	agreeableness
agreeing	disagreeable	disagreeably	disagreeableness
creatures	creates	created	recreation
creator	creative	creating	creatively
creativity	uncreative	creation	recreational

Lessons with More Complex Roots

Sometimes there are root words whose meaning must be taught so that students can see how words in that family are related in meaning. The most useful of these is the root word *port.*

Write the words *reporter, portable,* and *export* on the board. Pronounce the words as you underline *port* in each. Tell students that many words in English have the word *port* in them. Tell them to listen as you tell them some meaning for the three words on the board to see if they can hear a meaning all the words share.

A reporter carries a story back to tell others.
Something you can carry with you is portable.
When you export something, you take or carry it out of the country.

Help students to understand that *port* often means "carry or take." Next write this list of words on the board one at a time and help students to see how the meanings change but are still related to *port:*

port	import
export	importer
exportable	transport
nonexportable	transportation

Label this list of words *Carry/Take.*

Begin another list with the words *portion* and *portrait.* Underline *port.* Help students to see that not all words that have *port* in them have a meaning clearly related to *carry* or *take.* Tell students that when they see a word containing *port* whose meaning they do not know, they should try to figure out a meaning related to *take* or *carry* and see if that meaning makes sense in the sentence. Have students set up their paper in two columns like your board. Then call out some words, some of which have the meaning of *carry* or *take* and some of which don't. Here are some possibilities:

importer	exporter	airport	deport
unimportant	porter	portray	passport
misreport	support	nonsupport	opportunity
seaport	important	portfolio	Portugal

You could do a similar activity with the root *press.* Write the words *depression, impress,* and *repress* on the board. Pronounce the words as you underline *press* in each. Tell students that many words in English have the word *press* in them. Tell them to listen as you tell them some meanings for the words on the board to see if they can hear a meaning all the words share.

> "You make a depression when you push something down. You feel depression when you feel pushed down. When you repress a feeling, you push it out of your mind. You impress people when you push your good image into their minds."

Help students to understand that *press* often means "push." Next write these words on the board and help students to see how the meanings change but are still related to press:

press	oppress
express	oppressive
expressible	oppressiveness
inexpressible	

Tell students that when they see a word containing *press* whose meaning they do not know, they should try to figure out a meaning related to push and see if that meaning makes sense in the sentence they are reading.

Begin another column with the word *cypress*. Have students notice that *cypress* ends in *press* but there does not appear to be any "push" meaning in *cypress*. Here are some words, only one of which does not have any "push" meaning relationship.

expression	expressway	inexpressible	antidepressant
compression	pressure	pressurize	suppress
impressive	unimpressed	repressive	empress

Some other root words that are easy for students to understand and that have many related words are:

act: action, react, activity, active, inactive, activate
sign: signature, design, resign, designate, signal, insignia, significant
form: reform, inform, information, deform, uniform, formula, transform
meter: barometer, thermometer, kilometer, centimeter, millimeter, diameter

The Nifty Thrifty Fifty

All the activities described in this chapter so far will help children develop a store of big words they can read and spell, and teach them how to analyze big words for familiar patterns. Because a limited number of prefixes, suffixes, and spelling changes can be found in thousands of multisyllabic words, all children should have example words for these that are thoroughly familiar to them. What words could older children learn to read, spell, and analyze so that we could be sure they had examples for these common patterns?

I created such a list by deciding which prefixes, suffixes, and spelling changes were most prevalent in the multisyllabic words students might encounter. I included all the prefixes and suffixes determined to be most common in the White, Sowell, and Yanagihara study. Because I wanted to create a list that would provide the maximum help with all three big-word tasks, I added prefixes and suffixes such as *con/com, per, ex, ture, ian* not included in that study because they were not considered helpful from a meaning standpoint. These prefixes are, however, useful spelling and pronunciation chunks.

Having created the list of "transferable chunks," I then wanted to find the "most-apt-to-be-known" word containing each chunk. I consulted *The Living Word Vocabulary* (Dale & O'Rourke, 1981), which indicates for 44,000 words the grade level at which more than two-thirds of the students tested knew the meaning of the word. Because the test from which it was determined students knew the meanings also required them to read the word, it can also be inferred that at least two-thirds of the students could decode and pronounce the word. The goal was to find words that two-thirds of fourth graders could read and knew at least one meaning for. After much finagling, a list of 50 words was created that contains all the most useful prefixes, suffixes, and spelling changes. All but eight of these words were known by more than two-thirds of fourth graders. Seven words—*antifreeze, classify, deodorize, impression, irresponsible, prehistoric,* and *semifinal*—were not known by two-thirds of fourth graders but were known by two-thirds of sixth graders. *International,* the most known word containing the prefix *inter,* was known by two-thirds of eighth graders. Because this list of 50 words is apt to be known by so many intermediate-age and older students, and because it so economically represents all the important big-word parts, I named this list the Nifty Thrifty Fifty.

There are endless possibilities for how the list might be used. First, however, students must learn to spell the words. Teachers might want to start a word wall (see Chapter 6) of big words and add five words each week to the wall. They might take a few minutes each day to chant the spelling of the words and talk about the parts of the word that could be applied to other words. This talking should be as nonjargony as possible. Rather than talking about the root word *freeze* and the prefix *anti,* the discussions should be about how antifreeze keeps your car's engine from freezing up and, thus, it is protection against freezing. Students should be asked to think

The Nifty Thrifty Fifty

Word	Prefix	Suffix or ending
antifreeze	anti	
beautiful		ful (y-i)
classify		ify
communities	com	es (y-i)
community	com	
composer	com	er
continuous	con	ous
conversation	con	tion
deodorize	de	ize
different		ent
discovery	dis	y
dishonest	dis	
electricity		ity
employee	em	ee
encouragement	en	ment
expensive	ex	ive
forecast	fore	
forgotten		en (double t)
governor		or
happiness		ness (y-i)
hopeless		less
illegal	il	
impossible	im	
impression	im	sion
independence	in	ence
international	inter	al
invasion	in	sion
irresponsible	ir	ible
midnight	mid	
misunderstand	mis	
musician		ian
nonliving	non	ing (drop e)
overpower	over	
performance	per	ance
prehistoric	pre	ic
prettier		er (y-i)
rearrange	re	

Word	Prefix	Suffix or ending
replacement	re	ment
richest		est
semifinal	semi	
signature		ture
submarine	sub	
supermarkets	super	s
swimming		ing (double m)
transportation	trans	tion
underweight	under	
unfinished	un	ed
unfriendly	un	ly
unpleasant	un	ant
valuable		able (drop e)

of other words that look and sound like *antifreeze* and then decide if the *anti* parts of those words could have anything to do with the notion of "against."

> "What is an antibiotic against?" "What is an antiaircraft weapon?"

For suffixes, the discussion should center around how the suffix changes how the word can be used in a sentence.

> "A *musician* makes music. What does a beautician, electrician, physician, or magician do?"

> "When you need to replace something, you get a replacement. What do you get when someone encourages you?" "What do you call it when you accomplish something?"

Spelling changes should be noticed and applied to similar words.

> "*Communities* is the plural of *community*. How would you spell *parties*? *Candies*? *Personalities*?"

> "When we forget something, we say it was forgotten. How would you spell *bitten*? *Written*?"

If this list is to become truly useful to students, they need to learn to spell the words gradually over time, and they need to be shown how the patterns found in these words can be useful in decoding, spelling, and figuring out meaning for lots of other words. Here is an example of how the first words might be taught:

1. Explain that in English, many big words are just smaller words with prefixes and suffixes. The Nifty Thrifty Fifty words include all the important prefixes and suffixes and spelling changes needed to read, spell, and figure out meanings for thousands of other words.

2. Add 5–6 words to your display each week. Use different colors and make the words big and bold so that they are easily seen.

3. Have students chant each word cheerleader style with you. After cheering for each word, help students analyze the word, talking about meaning and determining the root, prefix, and suffix, and noting any spelling changes.

    composer—A composer is a person who composes something. Many other words such as *writer, reporter,* and *teacher* are made up of a root word and the suffix *er,* meaning a person or thing that does something.

    expensive—The word *expense* with the suffix *ive* added and the *e* in *expense* dropped. Another related word that students might not know is *expend.* You might be able to make the *expend-expense-expensive* relationship clear to them by using the sports terms *defend, defense, defensive.*

    encouragement—When you encourage someone, you give them encouragement. Many other words such as *argue, argument; replace, replacement* follow this same pattern. The root word for *encourage* is *courage.* So *encouragement* is made up of the prefix *en,* the root word *courage,* and the suffix *ment.*

    impossible—The root *possible* with the suffix *im.* In many words, including *impatient* and *immature,* the suffix *im* changes the word to an opposite.

    musician—A musician is a person who makes music. A beautician helps make you beautiful and a magician makes magic. *Musician* has the root word *music* with the suffix *ian,* which sometimes indicates the person who does something. There are no spelling changes, but the pronunciation changes. Have students say the words *music* and *musician, magic,* and *magician* and notice how the pronunciation changes.

4. Once you have noticed the composition for each word, helped students see other words that work in a similar way, and cheered for each word, have students write

each word. Students enjoy writing the words more and focus better on the word if you give clues to the word such as:

> Number 1 is the opposite of discouragement
>
> For number 2, write the word that tells what you are if you play the guitar.
>
> For number 3, write what you are if you play the guitar but you also make up the songs you play.
>
> Write the word that is the opposite of possible for number 4.
>
> The last word means costing a lot of money.

5. After students write all the words, have them check their own papers by once more chanting the letters aloud, underlining each as they say it.

When you have a few minute of "sponge" time, practice the words by chanting or writing. As you are cheering or writing each word, ask students to identify the root, prefix, and suffix and talk about how these affect the meaning of the root word. Point out any spelling changes.

The following week, add another five or six words and follow the foregoing procedures. When you have enough words, begin to show students how parts from the Nifty Thrifty Fifty words can be combined to spell lots of other words. From just the 11 words *composer, discovery, encouragement, expensive, hopeless, impossible, impression, musician, richest, transportation,* and *unfriendly,* students should be able to decode, spell, and discuss meanings for:

compose	pose	discover	encourage	courage
import	importation	possible	compress	compression
friendly	transpose	dispose	discourage	discouragement
enrich	enrichment	uncover	richly	hopelessly
impress	inexpensive	transport	port	expose
express	expression	export	exportation	

As more and more words are added, students become quite impressed with the number of transfer words they can read, spell, and build meanings for. (For more Nifty Thrifty Fifty lessons, see *Month-by-Month Phonics for Upper Grades* by Cunningham & Hall, 1998.)

Facility with big words is essential for students as they read, write, and learn in all areas of school and life. Many big words occur infrequently, but when they do occur, they carry a lot of the meaning and content of what is being read. English is a language in which many words are related through their morphology. Linguists estimate that every big word a child can read, spell, and analyze enables the reader to

Nifty Thrifty Fifty Transfer Words

Here are just some of the words buildable from just the parts of the 50 words. The number grows astronomically when the prefixes and suffixes are attached to other root words students know.

conform	conformity	inform	informer	informant
information	misinform	uninformed	formation	formal
transformation	transform	performer	responsibility	responsive
responsiveness	honesty	dishonesty	honestly	legally
illegally	responsibly	irresponsibly	arranging	rearranging
placing	replacing	misplacing	report	reporter
refinish	relive	refreeze	reclassify	revalue
recover	rediscover	electrical	displease	discontinue
disposal	musical	continual	employer	employment
unemployment	unemployed	employable	difference	unemployable
consignment	nationality	nationalities	internationalize	nationalize
interdependence	depress	depression	deodorant	deport
deportation	deportee	devalue	declassify	decompose
deform	deformity	prearrange	resign	resignation
designation	significant	significance	freezer	freezing
freezable	subfreezing	underclass	overexpose	underexpose
superimpose	undercover	forecaster	forecasting	forecastable
empowerment	miscast	overture	empower	antidepressant
powerful	powerfully	powerfulness	powerless	powerlessly
powerlessness	superpower	finalize	finalizing	finalization
weighty	weightless	beautician	electrician	undervalue
unfriendliness	friendlier	friendliest	friendliness	unpleasantness
historical	historically	expressive	impressive	repressive
invasive	noninvasive	invasiveness	hopefully	hopelessly

acquire six or seven other morphemically related words. Students who learn to look for patterns in the big new words they meet will be better spellers and decoders. If they learn to look further and consider possible meaning relationships, they will increase the size of their meaning vocabulary stores.

Making Big Words

You learned in Chapter Seven how to do Making Words lessons to help your students discover how our English spelling system works and how rhymes can help them decode and spell lots of other rhyming words. Making Big Words lessons help children learn how words are related through their morphemes—roots, prefixes, and suffixes—and how understanding these relationships helps them decode and spell other related words.

To do a Making Big Words lesson, we give students a strip of letters. We ask them to write the capital letters on the back and then tear the strip into letters. The letter strip is always alphabetical—vowels first and then consonants—so as not to give away the secret word.

Students are then directed to make 10–15 words, including the secret word that uses all the letters. Once the 10–15 words are made, the sort step of the lesson begins. The words are displayed on cards. Students read all the words in the order made. They are then asked to sort the related words. Related words are words that share a root word. As students sort the related words, they use these words in a sentence and explain how the words are related. Here are the words sorted in a lesson in which the secret word was *international:*

rot/rotten	rent/rental	alter/alteration
tolerant/intolerant	nation/national/international	

Students' explanations should focus on meaning and how the words are used in sentences:

"When something *rots,* we say it is *rotten.*"

"When you *rent* a car, you have a *rental* car."

"When you *alter* something, that's an *alteration.*"

"The opposite of *tolerant* is *intolerant.*"

"Problems that one nation has are *national* problems but problems between nations are *international.*"

The final step of a Making Big Words lesson is the transfer step. Students are asked to spell some words that are related in the same way as the sorted words. In this lesson they spell *hid/hidden, person/personal,* and *mission/intermission.*

Because students like to manipulate the letters and come up with their own words, we usually give them a take-home sheet with the same letters used in the lesson. The sheet has the letters across the top and blocks for writing words. Students write capital letters on the back and then cut the letters apart. They manipulate the letters to make words and then write them in the blocks. This is a popular homework assignment with students and their parents. When we write the letters at the top, we write them in alphabetical order—vowels and then consonants—so as not to give away the secret word. Students love being the "smart" ones who "know the secret word" and watching parents and other relatives try to figure it out.

A Sample Making Big Words Lesson

Here is an example of how a Making Big Words lesson might look. This lesson is adapted from *Big Words for Big Kids* (Cunningham, 2003), which contains 100 similar lessons focused on how words are related through their roots, prefixes, and suffixes. The students are given a strip with the following letters:

a	a	i	o	o	n	n	p	r	r	s	t	t	t

The teacher directs the students how many letters to use and what words to make. The teacher also gives a short oral sentence for each word. After each word is made, students are shown an index card with the correct spelling. The teacher checks to make sure everyone has fixed each word before going on the next word. The lesson is fast-paced to keep the attention of all the students.

1. Take three letters and spell **art.** "We hung our **art** in the halls."
2. Use four letters to spell **port.** "Sailors go to 'any **port** in a storm!' "
3. Use six letters to spell **artist.** "The **artist** was painting in the garden."
4. Use six letters to spell **nation.** "Our **nation** began in 1776."
5. Add a letter to spell **nations.** "The children come from many **nations.**"
6. Use seven letters to spell **airport.** "The **airport** is not far from my house."
7. Use seven letters to spell **patriot.** "A **patriot** is a person who supports the country."
8. Add a letter to spell **patriots.** "He was a quarterback with the New England **Patriots.**"
9. Use nine letters to spell **transport.** "His job was to **transport** the cars to the car dealers."
10. It's time for the secret word. (Wait one minute and then give clues if no one has figured it out.) Add your letters to *transport* to spell the secret word. "Cars, trucks, buses, trains, and planes are different kinds of **transportation.**"

Once the last word is made, the words on index cards are displayed and read together by the class.

| art | port | artist | nation | nations |
| airport | patriot | patriots | transport | transportation |

The teacher then asks the students to find and put together any related words. As related words are sorted out, the teacher and students talk about how the words are related and together they make up sentences that combine the related words.

art	nation	patriot	port
artist	nations	patriots	airport
			transport
			transportation

The transfer step helps students realize how the words made and sorted will help them to decode, spell, and build meaning for other words. The teacher names some related words and asks students to spell them and explain how they are related.

"Who can spell *cycle* and *cyclist* and make a sentence to show their relationship?"

"Who can spell *biology* and *biologist* and make a sentence to show their relationship?"

"Who can spell *inform* and *information* and make a sentence to show their relationship?"

"Who can spell *combine* and *combination* and make a sentence to show their relationship?"

As the words are spelled, the teacher writes the word on the board and helps students see the relationships between these words and the words they have just made and sorted.

Summary: How the Big Words Activities Are Multilevel

Throughout this book, I have emphasized that if we are going to succeed in teaching all children to read and write as well as they possibly can, we have to present them with activities that have "scope." Glancing back through the activities in the

Part Four chapters, you should see many opportunities for struggling readers to continue to develop their word knowledge and challenges for our advanced readers. Some big words are just "a little big" and others are "really big." By including a variety of words in all the activities, all levels of learners can learn what they are ready to learn and feel successful.

The issue of making sure to include something challenging for advanced readers is not generally a problem when helping children learn to decode, spell, and build meaning for big words. Even advanced readers often fail to notice morphemic relationships and take full advantage of the big words in their word stores. Teachers of older children who have done the activities described in these chapters have reported remarkable and rapid progress in the ability of their students to read and understand the sophisticated text they begin to encounter from late third grade and continuing through high school.

In the final part of this book, I will share with you some strategies teachers use for coaching children to use what they know when they need it—when they are actually reading and writing. I will also share some assessment devices that focus not just on what children know about phonics but also on what they actually use while reading and writing. Everything in *Phonics They Use* is grounded in the research literature and the pertinent research is summarized in Chapter Fourteen. The final chapter summarizes some of the major jargon teachers are expected to know. This chapter cautions you to not use too much of this jargon with your children because it tends to confuse them and take their attention away from what you are really trying to teach them. Teachers, however, are expected to know this jargon and the final chapter provides you with a handy reference.

Coaching, Assessment, Research, and Jargon

Coaching for Strategic Decoding and Spelling

If you have a typical class of students, you probably have children who know a lot more about letters, sounds, and spelling patterns than they actually use when reading and writing. A basic principle of *Phonics They Use* is that the work we do with words is only useful and worthwhile if children actually use what they know while reading and writing. In all word activities, we stress transfer to reading and writing. In Guess the Covered Word activities, we emphasize helping children verbalize how using meaning, all the beginning letters, and word length helps them make a very good guess. By ending each and every Making Words and Rounding Up the Rhymes lesson with a few transfer words that the rhyming words will help children read and spell, we are constantly reminding them how and when to use their word strategies. Children write using words used in Reading/Writing Rhymes and What Looks Right? lessons. In spite of all this concerted effort, there are

162

some obstinate children who "just don't get it!" All the activities in the big-words chapters focus children on how looking for familiar chunks, roots, prefixes, and suffixes helps them decode, spell, and build meaning for big words.

In spite of all our good efforts at transfer during the big-words activities, some children participate, enjoy, and even seem to understand our word activities but when they read and write, they don't use what they know! To help children use whatever phonics they know, we seize opportunities to coach during writing conferences and we meet with children one-on-one or in small coaching groups and coach them to use what they know to figure out new words.

Coaching during Writing Conferences

Writing conferences—when we are helping children revise, edit, and fix their spelling on a piece they are going to publish—provide an opportunity to coach children to use what we know they have learned about spelling. When we publish a book or prepare pieces for display on the bulletin board, we help children to spell the words correctly so that other people can read what they wrote. There are many words that children use in their writing that they can't be expected to know how to spell and, when we are conferencing with them, we simply acknowledge the good efforts shown in their attempts at spelling and then write the correct spelling of the words. But at other times, we use the writing conference as the teachable moment to nudge them forward in their use of spelling patterns. Imagine that you are editing with a child and the child has written the word *trade* as *trd*. Ask that child:

> "Where's your vowel? Every word needs at least one vowel. Remember in Making Words we always use at least one red letter in every word. Stretch out the word *trade* and listen for the vowel you hear."

The child will probably hear the *a*. Then help him decide where to put it. Add the *e* on the end and tell him that you can't hear the *e* but that if you say *trade* slowly, you can hear the *a* and that when he is trying to spell a word to remember that every word needs at least one vowel.

Now imagine that another child comes to you with *trade* spelled "*trad.*" You might say something like:

> "That was a good try on *trade.* You wrote down every sound you heard. But let's look at the spelling pattern *a-d.* We know some a-d words: *b-a-d* spells *bad; m-a-d* spells *mad;* d-a-d spells *dad.* Can you think of a word that rhymes with *trade* and uses that spelling pattern?"

If *made* is on the word wall, the child will probably realize that *trade* should be spelled with the same pattern. It is also possible (but not likely) that he will think of *paid* and want to spell *trade* t-r-a-i-d. In this case, point out that *trade* does rhyme with *paid* and could be spelled like *paid* but point out the other pattern in words like *made* and *grade*.

Here is another common example. The child has written *invitation* spelled "invitashun." You need to compliment the child for listening for all the sounds in the word but then remind the child that big words often have chunks that are spelled differently. If you have a *tion* word on the word wall—such as *question* or *vacation*—call that child's attention to that word and help her use the last chunk to spell *invitation* correctly. If you don't have a *tion* word on the word wall, try to think of a *tion* word the child might be able to spell—perhaps *nation* or *motion*. You might also consider adding a *tion* word to the word wall and doing on-the-back activities in which the children use the *tion* word-wall word to spell simple two-syllable words such as *nation, motion, lotion, mention,* and *caption*.

Writing conferences are a great opportunity to individualize what we teach children. For some children, we simply praise their correct spelling of word-wall words, encourage their invented spelling efforts, and fix the spelling. For other children, we use the opportunity to point out things about letters, sounds, and spelling patterns that they know when doing words but are not applying as they are writing.

Coaching during Reading

To coach children to use what they know while reading, we do some short (5–10 minutes) individual or very small group coaching sessions in which we lead them through the steps at the exact moment they need to use them. We use text that they haven't read before and that is going to contain some words they need to figure out. Having text at instructional level (5–10 errors per 100 words) is ideal. Explain to the children that the book will have words they haven't learned yet and that the purpose of these lessons is to practice how good readers figure out words they don't know. Have a child begin reading and when the child comes to an unknown word and stops, say:

"Put your finger on the word and say all the letters."

Good readers look at all the letters in each word. Children who are struggling with reading tend to look quickly at the word and, if they don't instantly recognize it, they stop and wait for someone to tell them the word. Asking them to say all the letters forces them to look at all the letters. (Note that we are not giving the sounds of letters but rather naming the letters.) Sometimes, after saying all the letters, they correctly pronounce the word! This is proof that they aren't in the habit of looking at all the letters and you should let them know what they have done by saying something like:

> "That's right. There are lots of words we see when we are reading that we don't recognize right away but, when we look at all the letters, we can sometimes figure them out. Good job! Continue reading."

If, after saying the letters, the child does not say the word, you should say:

> "Keep your finger on that word and finish the sentence."

It may seem foolish to have the child keep his or her finger there but young children's print tracking skills are not nearly as good as ours. Many children can't use the context of the sentence and the letters in the unknown word to figure out a word because, once they get to the end of the sentence, they can't quickly look back and find the troublesome word. Keeping one finger on the word allows the child to quickly track back. If, after finishing the sentence, the child correctly pronounces the word, say something like:

> "Right. You can figure out lots of words you don't know if you use your finger to keep track of where the word is, finish the sentence, and then do like we do in Guess the Covered Word and guess a word that makes sense, begins with all the right letters, and is the right length. Continue reading."

If the child still does not get the word, you have four possible cues to point out. If there is a good picture clue (which the child has ignored!), you could say,

> "What animal do you see in the picture that begins with *l*?"

If the troublesome word can be decoded based on one of the patterns on the word wall or used frequently during other word activities, you could say,

> "Let's see. The word is spelled s-t-r-i-n-g. We know that t-h-i-n-g spells *thing*. Can you make this word rhyme with *thing*?"

If the word has more than eight letters, you can ask the child to chunk it and see if he or she recognizes any familiar chunks.

> "The word is spelled *c-a-r-e-f-u-l-l-y*. Do you recognize a root word or other chunk you know?"

If there is nothing in the picture to help and the word is not easily decodable based on a familiar rhyming word, you can give an explicit context clue. Imagine that the troublesome word is *place* in the sentence:

Clifford wanted to go to a faraway place.

You could say:

"Where do you think Clifford might want to go to that begins with p-l?"

If the child gets the word after you give the most appropriate cue, be sure to tell the child what he or she did.

"Right. Lots of times there is something in the picture that matches a word we don't know and if we use the picture and the letters and making sense, we can figure out the word."

Or:

"Right. You can use words that rhyme with words you know to help you figure out lots of words just like we do on the back of our word-wall paper and when we figure out new words at the end of Making Words or Rounding Up the Rhymes."

Or:

"Right. You saw the root word *care* and then you noticed the chunks *ful* and *ly* and blended them all together to come up with the word."

Or:

"Right. When you thought about where Clifford might go and the sound for the letters *p-l, place* was a word with all the beginning letters that made sense."

The tactics described so far will result in the reader figuring out an unknown word about 90 percent of the time. But there is always a word that they still don't get and if we tell them the word, we are reinforcing their "wait and she will tell me eventually" decoding strategy. We never tell them the word but, finally, when all else has failed, we will give them a choice from which they can't fail to get the word. Imagine that the word is *ridiculous* in the sentence:

That is a ridiculous hat.

We say to the child:

> "Well, let's see. Do you think it says, 'That is a ripe hat' or 'that is a ridiculous hat'?"

We make our alternative begin with the correct letters but be so unmeaningful that the child will make the right choice. We then say,

> "Good. That was a hard word but you got it! Let's continue reading."

Explaining this in writing makes it sound much longer and more complicated than it actually is. When we are coaching a child to learn to use what he or she knows (but isn't using), we choose text in which the child is going to come to an unknown word every second or third sentence. When the child stops at a word, we go through the following steps:

1. Put your finger on the word and say all the letters.
2. Keep your finger there and finish the sentence.
3. For the third clue, we pick the one of four that we think has the most potential to help the child figure out the word. We use only one of these four possible prompts.

   > "What do you see in the picture that starts with —?"

   Or:

   > "Let's see. The word is spelled —. We can spell —. Can you make this rhyme with —?"

   Or:

   > "Are there any root words or chunks you recognize?"

   Or:

   > "Where do you think Clifford would go that starts with —?"

4. Finally, if the cueing fails:

   > "Let's see. Do you think it says, 'That is a ridiculous hat' or 'that is a ripe hat'?"

When the child gets the word after any of our cueing, we congratulate the child and point out what strategy the child used that helped him or her figure out the word. If a child miscalls a word (instead of the usual struggling reader strategy of stopping on the word and waiting to be told), we wait for the child to finish the sentence, repeat the sentence as the child read it, point out that it didn't make sense, and then take the child through as many steps as necessary.

Most children do not need the kind of one-on-one or very small group coaching described here, but for those who do, short coaching sessions held a few times each week make a world of difference in children's ability to use what they know when they need to use it!

 # Summary

Phonics is only helpful to children if they use it when they need it—to figure out how to spell words while writing and decode words while reading. Many children will learn how to use what they know if you make sure to do the transfer parts of all the activities in this book. Some children need additional help to use what they know. Coaching children during writing conferences and in small groups or one-on-one sessions will ensure that phonics accomplishes its purpose with all the children we teach.

chapter 13

Assessment

Assessment is part of everything we do in life. Most of us make an assessment of the weather each morning to decide what to wear. We assess the food, service, and atmosphere as we dine at the new restaurant in town. We assess our new neighbors as we watch them interact with each other and move their furniture in. In this chapter, we will provide some examples of how you can make assessment an extension of your teaching—rather than just one more thing that has to be done.

What Is Assessment?

Sometimes it is easier to define something by beginning with what it is not. Assessment is not grading—although assessment can help you determine and support the grades you give. Assessment is not standardized test scores—although these scores can give you some general idea of what children have achieved so far. Assessment is collecting and analyzing data to make decisions about how children are performing and growing. Caldwell (2002) describes four steps for assessment. First, we must identify what we want to assess. Second, we collect evidence. Next, we analyze that evidence. Finally, we make a decision and act on that decision.

Assessment is an ongoing process for experienced teachers who have become good kid watchers. As the children respond to the various activities, teachers notice who can do what. Write down what you notice and you have anecdotal records! Samples—particularly writing samples and audiotaped samples of children reading—are also informative. By comparing samples done across time, growth can be determined and validated. Here are some ideas for ongoing assessment of children's phonics and spelling development.

Assessing Early Reading Behaviors

Print Concepts

One essential part of the foundation for learning to read is the ability to track print. Children who can track print can point to words, starting on the left and going from left to right. They then make a return sweep and track across the next line of print. They can match words by pointing to each word as they read. Another important concept for learning to read is understanding the jargon of print. When asked, they can point to the first word and the last word and the first letter and the last letter. These print concepts are essential to successfully beginning the journey toward literacy and, thus, are some of the most important concepts to assess during the first month of school.

Phonological and Phonemic Awareness

Children who have phonological awareness know what words are. They can tell you how many words are in a spoken sentence. They can clap syllables in words and know that the word *motorcycles* takes more claps than the word *car*. Children who have phonemic awareness can manipulate words. They can stretch out words and tell you what word you have said when you stretch one out. They can tell you that *bike* rhymes with *Mike* and that *book* doesn't. They can make up silly rhymes for objects in the classroom. They can segment words into their component sounds and blend sounds back together and identify the blended word.

We would assess their phonemic awareness by observing their ability to do rhyming word, blending, and segmenting tasks as we are doing the activities with the whole class. Just as for print concepts, we would require two pluses on two different days before deciding they had developed the concept. Phonemic awareness is not a single concept and is not an easy concept for many children. Not all children will have all parts of it even after several months, and we would know which ones needed continued nudges toward developing this as we moved into more advanced decoding and spelling activities.

Hallie Yopp (1995) published an excellent test of children's ability to segment words into sounds. You can find it in Volume 49 of *The Reading Teacher,* pages 20–29.

Word Learning

If you sit down with children on the first day of school and try to determine if they can read by giving them a simple book to read or testing them on some common words such as *the, and, of,* or *with,* you would probably conclude that most children can't read yet. But many children enter school with some known words. The words they know are usually "important to them" concrete words. Knowing 10–15 words is important not because you can read much with these few words, but because in learning these first words, you have accomplished a critical task. Children who come to school already able to read or write some concrete words have accomplished an important and difficult task. They have learned how to learn words.

All children should have learned some words from the reading and writing activities described in Part One. To assess their word learning, you may want to check their ability to read the names of the children in the class, some of the most interesting words from favorite Big Books and predictable charts. For children who came already knowing some concrete words, you may want to see if they have learned some of the high-frequency words—such as *like, is, in,* and *the*—often repeated in the Big Books and predictable charts. The expectation should not be that anyone is learning all words (although your children who came already reading will astound you with how little repetition they require to learn a word!), but that everyone is adding some words to their store of words they can read.

Letter Names and Sounds

We assess their letter name and sound knowledge by showing them a sheet containing all the letters in upper- and lowercase form and asking them to point to any letters they know. Children look over the sheet and find some they know and we note these on their record sheet with an *n* for *name.* Once they have done this, we point to some of the letters they didn't name and ask:

"Can you tell me what sound this letter makes?"

If they give us an appropriate sound, we indicate this with an *s* for *sound* on their record sheet.

Next, we point to some of the letters they haven't identified and ask:

"Do you know any words that begin with this letter?"

We indicate with a *w* for *word* any letters they didn't give us names or sounds for but for which they do have a word association.

Checklists

Many teachers of young children keep a checklist such as the example given here. Each day, they put the checklists of two or three children on their clipboard and observe and talk with these children as they are engaged in reading and writing to determine how they are developing the critical behaviors. Teachers often use a simple system of putting a minus (−) to indicate the child does not have that behavior; a question mark (?) when the behavior is erratic or it is unclear that the child has it; and a plus (+) to indicate the child does seem to have developed that behavior. Three pluses on three different dates are a reliable indicator that that child has indeed developed that behavior.

 # Assessing Word Strategies

As children move from the early reading stages into more independent reading and writing stages, we need to monitor and assess their development of sight words and decoding and spelling strategies. This book contains many activities for developing these strategies. Our assessment, however, must take place while the children are actually reading and writing. The goal of word instruction is to teach children words and strategies they actually use when they are reading and writing. What we want to know is not how children spell words during the daily word-wall activity but how quickly they recognize these words when they are reading and how correctly they spell these words when they are writing.

There are many opportunities throughout the day to make these observations. As children are engaged in self-selected reading, we can ask them to read aloud a page or two. As they read, we listen for how fluently they read, how automatically they identify the word-wall words, and how they use patterns, context, and other cues to figure out unknown words. When children are reading in partners, we can circulate to the different partnerships and ask them to read a page to us. Again, we can note how they use what we are teaching them about words as they actually read text. Another opportunity to observe their sight word, word identification, and fluency behaviors is when we meet with small coaching groups.

Beginning Reading Strategies

Name _____   Dates Checked (− ? +)

Tracks Print   — — — — — — —
    left page first
    top to bottom
    left to right
    return sweep
    points to each word

Knows reading "jargon"   — — — — — — —
    identifies one letter, one word, and one sentence
    identifies first word, first and last letters in a word

Demonstrates phonological awareness   — — — — — — —
    counts words
    claps syllables

Demonstrates phonemic awareness   — — — — — — —
    stretches out words when attempting to spell
    blends and segments words
    identifies and produces rhymes

Reads some words   — — — — — — —
    names of children in the class
    interesting words from shared reading and charts
    high-frequency words from shared reading and charts

Demonstrates alphabet awareness   — — — — — — —
    names some letters
    knows some words that begin with certain letters
    knows some common letter sounds

Date _____ Observations:

Date _____ Observations:

Date _____ Observations:

We observe their spelling behaviors by periodically looking at samples of their first-draft writing, by analyzing their spelling in writing samples we collect three times each year, and in our revising, editing, publishing conferences with individual children.

Observing Word Strategies in Reading

By observing children's reading, teachers can look at the errors children make and determine what word identification strategies they are using. Good readers will self-correct many of their errors. This usually indicates that they are using context to check that what they are reading makes sense. Successful self-correction is an excellent indicator that the reader is using all three cueing systems—meaning (semantic), sounding like language (syntactic), and letter–sound knowledge (graphophonic). Some readers tend to overuse context—their errors make sense but don't have most of the letter–sound relationships of the original word. Others overuse letter–sound knowledge. Their errors look and sound a lot like the original words but they don't make any sense. By observing children's reading, we can determine what strategies they are using and what kind of instructional activities we might provide for them.

To look at children's word strategies while reading, we first must have something for them to read in which they make some but not too many errors. This level is generally referred to as the instructional level—the level of a book or story in which the child correctly identifies at least 90–95 percent of the words and has adequate comprehension of what was read. The text the child is reading should be something the child has not read before and, although the child may read more than 100 words, the first 100 words are generally used for analysis.

Teachers use a variety of materials to do this assessment, depending on what is available and what the school system requires. Some teachers use passages contained in the assessment package that accompanies many basal reading series. Other teachers/schools have designated certain "real" books as benchmark books. They don't use these books for instruction but only for assessment purposes. They decide that one book is what most first graders could read at the 90–95 percent word identification accuracy level early in the year. Another book represents the middle of first-grade difficulty level and a third book is selected as being at the end of first-grade level. Finally, some teachers use a published Informal Reading Inventory, which contains graded passages beginning at preprimer level and going through sixth grade.

Regardless of what you use, the procedures are the same. You have the children read the text you think will be at instructional level. This text should be text the children have not had a chance to read before and they should be told that you cannot help them while reading. When they get to a word they don't know, they should be told "do the best they can to figure it out" because you can't tell them any words. Also tell them that they should think about what they are reading because they will be asked to tell in their own words what the text they read was about after they read it.

As each child reads, we take an oral reading record. If we have made a copy of the text (or if we are using a passage from a basal assessment or an Informal Reading Inventory), we mark right on the passage. If not, we simply record on a sheet of paper. We use a simple marking system and we only score the first 100 words.

Put a check mark over each word read correctly.
If the child misreads a word (*grows* for *growls*), write the error above it.
If the child leaves a word out, circle that word.
If the child self-corrects, write *SC* above it. *SC* words are counted as correct.
If the child makes the same error more than once, only count it one time.

After the child has read the passage, have the child close the book (or take the passage away) and ask the child to tell what the text was about. Ask questions as needed to determine that the child understood at least 70–80 percent of the information read. We consider passages in which the child's word identification accuracy is in the 90–95 percent range, and comprehension is at least 70–80 percent, to be at the instructional level of the child. When we have recorded the oral reading of a child at instructional level, we can then analyze the child's errors and self-corrections to determine what word strategies the child is actually using.

Observing Word Strategies in Writing

Writing samples also show growth in word knowledge. Because writing results in a visible, external product, it is easier to determine what they are actually using. By looking at two or three writing samples done a month or more apart, progress in word development is easy to determine. In looking at their writing sample to determine their level of word knowledge, we want to look at their spelling of high-frequency words and their attempts at spelling less frequent words. First, we notice whether all the word-wall words are spelled correctly. Next, we look at how the child is spelling words on the wall and not readily available in the room. Do their invented spellings indicate that they can hear sounds in words and know what letters usually represent those sounds? Are the letters in the correct order? Are they beginning to spell by pattern rather than just putting down one letter for each sound? Are they using starred word-wall words to spell rhyming words? Are they adding endings correctly and beginning to use appropriate spelling changes?

In addition to writings on self-selected topics, many schools collect focused writing samples and look at these to determine growth in writing ability and word knowledge. A focused writing sample collected for assessment purposes should have a topic specified about which most children have good general knowledge. Children should write on this topic with no assistance from the teacher or any other child. Some examples of topics used in primary classrooms include:

"My Favorite Things to Do"
"What I Like to Do at School"
"An Animal I Would Like to Have for a Pet"

Many schools have the child write about the same topic at several different points in time—May of kindergarten, January and May of first grade, and January and May of second grade, for example. These topic-focused, nonassisted first drafts are then compared to determine an individual child's writing growth. In addition to a slew of valuable information about how the child writes—sentence sense, topic sense, word choice, writing conventions, and so on—these samples yield valuable information about the child's developing word knowledge.

As with early reading behaviors, the "– ? +" system allows us to easily record what we observe on each child's word behavior checklist.

The Names Test

A final possibility to consider when assessing children's word knowledge is the Names Test. I developed the Names Test several years ago when working with a group of older remedial readers. These boys were good context users, and it was quite difficult to determine what they knew about letter–sound patterns when they were reading contextually because they were such good context users. I wanted a measure of their word identification ability that was not confounded by context but that was not just a list of words. Reading a list of words is a rather unnatural act, and choosing the words is quite difficult. If you choose words most children have in their listening vocabularies, you run the risk of also choosing words they know as sight words and thus don't have to decode, and you could overestimate their letter–sound knowledge. If you choose very obscure words, the children probably don't have the words in their listening vocabularies and thus can't use the "sounds right" clue to check their probable pronunciation.

Imagine that you want to know whether a child can decode words with the common sound for the vowel *a*. If you have the child pronounce common words such as *clay, back,* and *star* to determine their ability to decode words with the vowel *a* and

Sight Word, Decoding, and Spelling Behaviors

Name _____ Dates Checked (– ? +)

Identifies word-wall words automatically
when reading   — — — — — — — —

Spells word-wall words correctly in
first-draft writing   — — — — — — — —

Uses letter patterns and picture and sentence
cues to decode   — — — — — — — —
> beginning letters of word (*br, sh, f*)
> rhyming pattern (*at, ight, ain*)
> endings (*s, ed, ing*)
> prefixes (*un, inter*) suffixes (*able, tion*) for big words
> combines letter cues, picture cues, and sentence cues

Uses letter patterns to spell words   — — — — — — —
> beginning letters of word (*br, sh, f*)
> rhyming pattern (*at, ight, ain*)
> endings (*s, ed, ing, er, est*)
> prefixes (*un, inter*) suffixes (*able, tion*) for big words

Self-monitors   — — — — — — —
> self-corrects when meaning is distorted
> self-corrects when nonsense word is produced
> rereads to correct phrasing
> rereads for fluency

Reads fluently   — — — — — — —
> with phrasing
> attending to punctuation
> with expression

Writes fluently   — — — — — — —
> words are written quickly
> handwriting is not slow and laborious
> focused on meaning

they correctly pronounce them, you don't know whether they decoded those words or if these were sight words learned from their previous reading. For this reason, some tests use nonsense words to test decoding skills. The child might be asked to pronounce made-up words such as *glay, dack,* and *smar.* Nonsense words solve the problem of the child's knowing the words as sight words but nonsense words have another problem. While reading, good readers ask themselves questions such as "Did that make sense?" and "Did that sound right?" Asking these questions is a very important reading strategy because it allows the readers to self-correct errors and to constantly check their decoding with the context of what they are reading. Reading nonsense words violates this self-checking strategy good readers use and many good readers will mispronounce the nonsense words by making them into real words they have heard of. *Glay* might be pronounced as *"gray"* or *"glad." Dack* might be *"back"* or *"deck." Smar* might be pronounced *"smart."* Because children tend to want to make nonsense words into "words they have heard of," tests that use nonsense words often result in children showing less phonics ability than they actually have.

There is one type of word, however, which children hear often—and thus have in their listening vocabularies—but which they don't read often and thus are not apt to have already learned as sight words. Names are heard all over the place. Names are a big part of every TV and radio program, and usually these names are pronounced but not read. Names are one type of word that most children have a lot more of in their listening vocabularies than in their sight vocabularies; thus, names can be used to measure decoding ability not confounded by context.

In addition to their more-often-heard-than-read quality, names have another advantage for a word-reading test. We do sometimes read lists of names. Teachers and others often "call the roll." Thus, reading a list is a somewhat more natural real-reading task than most other word-list reading tasks. The Names Test (Cunningham, 1990; Duffelmeyer et al., 1994) was developed to help teachers reliably assess decoding ability using a real-life reading task.

Administering the Names Test

Print the names on index cards or copy the reproducible list in Figure 13.1. Make another list on which you can record responses. (See Figure 13.2.)

Ask the child to pretend that he or she is a teacher and that this is the list of names of the students in the class. Have the child read the list, as if the child is taking attendance.

Use a check to indicate correct responses and write the phonetic spelling for any incorrect responses given by a child. If a child does not attempt a name, write "no" next to that name and encourage the child to continue. For polysyllabic words, consider the word correct regardless of where the child places the accent on the word.

Jay Conway

Kimberly Blake

Cindy Sampson

Stanley Shaw

Flo Thornton

Ron Smitherman

Bernard Pendergraph

Austin Sheperd

Joan Brooks

Tim Cornell

Roberta Slade

Chester Wright

Wendy Swain

Dee Skidmore

Troy Whitlock

Shane Fletcher

Bertha Dale

Gene Loomis

Chuck Hoke

Homer Preston

Ginger Yale

Glen Spencer

Grace Brewster

Vance Middleton

Floyd Sheldon

Neal Wade

Thelma Rinehart

Yolanda Clark

Gus Quincy

Patrick Tweed

Fred Sherwood

Ned Westmoreland

Zane Anderson

Dean Bateman

Jake Murphy

FIGURE 13.1
Reproducible List of Names for the Names Test

Analyze the child's responses, looking for patterns indicative of decoding strengths and weaknesses. Keep a record of each child's responses and give the test again after several weeks or months of instruction as an indicator of growth in the ability to decode words.

_____ Jay	_____ Conway		
_____ Kimberly	_____ Blake		
_____ Cindy	_____ Sampson		
_____ Stanley	_____ Shaw		
_____ Flo	_____ Thornton		
_____ Ron	_____ Smitherman		
_____ Bernard	_____ Pendergraph		
_____ Austin	_____ Sheperd		
_____ Joan	_____ Brooks		
_____ Tim	_____ Cornell		
_____ Roberta	_____ Slade		
_____ Chester	_____ Wright		
_____ Wendy	_____ Swain		
_____ Dee	_____ Skidmore		
_____ Troy	_____ Whitlock		
_____ Shane	_____ Fletcher		
_____ Bertha	_____ Dale		
_____ Gene	_____ Loomis		
_____ Chuck	_____ Hoke		
_____ Homer	_____ Preston		
_____ Ginger	_____ Yale		
_____ Glen	_____ Spencer		
_____ Grace	_____ Brewster		
_____ Vance	_____ Middleton		
_____ Floyd	_____ Sheldon		
_____ Neal	_____ Wade		
_____ Thelma	_____ Rinehart		
_____ Yolanda	_____ Clark		
_____ Gus	_____ Quincy		
_____ Patrick	_____ Tweed		
_____ Fred	_____ Sherwood		
_____ Ned	_____ Westmoreland		
_____ Zane	_____ Anderson		
_____ Dean	_____ Bateman		
_____ Jake	_____ Murphy		

FIGURE 13.2
Names Response Sheet

Summary

Assessment is a part of everything we do. To make any kind of decision, we collect and analyze evidence and then act on that evidence. In assessing children's phonics and spelling knowledge, we must be sure that we focus more on what they use than what they know. This chapter has shared a variety of ways to observe children's reading and writing behaviors and to determine what phonics knowledge they have and how they use that knowledge. Recording and analyzing your findings will allow you to pick and choose from the activities described throughout this book and modify them as necessary for the children you teach.

chapter 14

The Theory and the Research—The Why Underlying the How

The question of instruction in phonics has aroused a lot of controversy. Some educators have held to the proposition that phonetic training is not only futile and wasteful but also harmful to the best interests of a reading program. Others believe that since the child must have some means of attacking strange words, instruction in phonics is imperative. There have been disputes also relative to the amount of phonics to be taught, the time when the teaching should take place and the methods to be used. In fact, the writer knows of no problem around which more disputes have centered.

Paul McKee (1934, p. 191)

Clearly, the phonics question has been plaguing the field of reading for a long time. In this chapter, I will share with you my own history as a student, a teacher, and a researcher with the phonics dilemma, review the major research findings of the past 40 years, and explain the relationship between the research and the type of phonics instruction found in this book.

My Personal Phonics History

My fate was probably sealed in 1949 when I was a first grader at High Street School in Westerly, Rhode Island. In the morning, we were divided into reading groups and read about the adventures of Sally, Dick, Jane, Puff, and Spot. After lunch each day, we all pulled out bright blue phonics books and sounded out words. Little did I know that at five years old, I was thrust right into the middle of the sight word/phonics controversy.

The year 1965 found me teaching first grade in Key West, Florida. I taught the phonics in my basal manual, and most children learned to distinguish short vowels from long vowels. The children in my top group even developed the ability to "sound out" new words, although even then I didn't quite believe that what they did when they came to a new word was in any way related to what I was teaching them about phonics. One day I overheard a boy remark to a friend,

"The short vowels are pretty short but the long ones look pretty short, too."

His friend then proceeded to explain it to him.

"It's simple. The little ones are the short ones and the capital ones are the long ones!"

Although I continued to teach first grade and the vowel rules for several years, my faith in them was badly shaken!

I got my master's degree in reading from Florida State in 1968. "Linguistics" was the buzzword at that time, and I thought that "linguistic readers" were going to solve the decoding problems of our poor readers. I got a chance to try this out with a fourth-grade class of poor readers. Armed with the Merrill Linguistic Readers and the SRA Basic Reading Series, I abandoned phonics rules for linguistic patterns. Things went pretty well for the first month. The students learned all the short *a* patterns and read about Dan in his tan van. As we moved on, however, they began to confuse the previously learned patterns with the new ones. Worse yet, I realized that the children had stopped trying to make sense of what they were reading and were simply sounding out the patterns!

By 1970, context was the only remaining tool in my decoding arsenal. "Say 'blank' and read the rest of the sentence and then go back and think about what would make sense," was my 1970 brand of decoding instruction. In 1971, I found myself in Terre Haute, Indiana, as the special reading teacher at the Indiana State University Laboratory School. All day I worked with poor readers. Mostly, I tried to get these students to enjoy reading and to talk about what they read. I did almost no phonics instruction, but it did worry me that almost all the poor readers had little ability to decode an unfamiliar word.

My "real challenges" arrived after lunch each day. Rod and Erin were sixth graders of normal intelligence who had been in remedial reading since second grade and who read at the second-grade level. Both boys were fluent with all the high-frequency words and were excellent users of picture and context clues. They could understand anything they could read and most of what you read to them. They had been scheduled for 45 minutes alone with me each day because they were to go on to the junior high next year and their parents were very worried that, after all these years, they still hadn't "caught on to reading."

For both Rod and Erin, the problem was clear-cut. They knew what reading was and that you were to make meaning from it. They enjoyed being read to and even enjoyed reading the high-interest, low-vocabulary books I could find that they could read themselves. They simply had not learned to decode! For the first semester, I taught Rod and Erin "word families." They were very competitive and I made Go Fish, Old Maid, and Concentration games, which they could win by matching and saying rhyming words. We also made charts of rhyming words and wrote jingles and riddles, which were awful but appealed to their sixth-grade silliness. In addition to rhyming games and writing rhymes, each day we read together and I reminded them of the one strategy I had taught them. Both boys knew that when you came to a short word you didn't know, you should look to see if it would rhyme with a word you did know. When they couldn't think of a rhyming word, I prompted them with one. They used this strategy when they were reading and were amazed to discover that they could figure out even unusual names—*Tran, Clark, Kurt.*

Unfortunately, their newfound decoding ability did not transfer to bigger words. I taught them a few simple syllable-division rules and they could sometimes figure out a two-syllable word, the syllables of which were familiar rhyming patterns—*zinger, target, pastor.* If a word had more than six letters, however, they couldn't even begin to do anything with it and would just skip it and go on!

By March, the boys were reading at a strong third-grade level—sometimes fourth—if they knew a lot about the topic. I knew that their inability and unwillingness to decode long words was the remaining hurdle, but I didn't know how to teach them to figure them out. I taught them some prefixes and suffixes and this helped with some words. I would drive home in the afternoons and see a big word on a billboard and ask myself,

"How did I figure out that word?"

I knew that I had not applied syllabication rules and then sounded out each syllable, but I didn't know what I had done.

We were at six weeks before the end of sixth grade and Rod and Erin had begun the countdown to summer and junior high! In desperation, I searched the Education Index for "polysyllabic word instruction." I didn't find much, and discounted most of what I did find. Context was what Rod and Erin were currently using. Syllabication rules weren't working (and research confirmed that!). They had learned many of the common prefixes and suffixes but they didn't seem to use them. Finally, one article suggested teaching students to use the dictionary respelling key. "Well, that's something I haven't tried," I thought. "But, no one is ever going to stop reading and find the word in the dictionary and use the respelling key," I argued with myself.

But I decided to do it. What did I have to lose? We had to do something useful for the last six weeks, and at least they would know how to use the respelling key to pronounce a word if they would take the time to do it. For two weeks, I taught them how to use the key to figure out the pronunciation of unknown words. Then, when they understood how to do it, I gave them each a different list of five "really long" words (*conscientious, filibuster, mannequin, Phoenician, sporadically*) each day. Before we could go on to do anything interesting, they each had to find their words and use the key to figure them out and pronounce them for me.

They hated it but "it was good for them," and I was determined that they would have a big-word tool to take with them to junior high, so each day, they came in and picked up their list and their dictionaries and went to work. Ten days before the end of school, Rod walked in and picked up his list of five "humongous" words and his dictionary. He began to look up the first word, then he stopped, looked at the word, and then looked at me. "What if I already know this word? Do I still have to look it up?" he asked.

"Well no," I responded. "I'm trying to give you a tool so that you can always pronounce any big word you ever come to, but if you know the word, you don't need the respelling key, do you?"

Rod looked again at the first word, studying the letters. He then correctly pronounced "spontaneous!" "That's right!" I exclaimed. "Now, you only have four to look up!" "Not if I know some of the others," Rod asserted. He was able to pronounce two of the other four words and only had to look up and use the key for two of the five big words. Meanwhile, Erin was studying his five words and he managed to pronounce two of his, only having to look up three. I was astonished! "Where had they learned those words?" I wondered. For the remaining nine days of school, Rod and Erin competed to see how many words they could figure out and not have to look up. To my amazement, by the last day of school they had gotten quite good at figuring out words of four or more syllables. The respelling key, which I had taught them to use as a tool, had taught them a system for independently figuring out big words. At the time I didn't understand how this miracle had occurred, but I sent Rod and Erin off to junior high more confident of their success than I had ever thought possible.

In 1972, I arrived at the University of Georgia to work on my doctorate in reading. I took my first seminar, and Dr. Ira Aaron led us to do some initial thinking about a dissertation topic. I already knew what I wanted to find out: "How do we decode an unknown word and particularly an unknown big word?" After much reading, thinking, and discussions with other doctoral students and Dr. George Mason, my advisor, I became convinced that decoding took place in what I called a compare/contrast way. Later this would be called "decoding by analogy." In addition to my dissertation (Cunningham, 1975–76), I did quite a bit of research into analogic decoding (Cunningham, 1979, 1980; Cunningham & Guthrie, 1982; Gaskins, Downer, Anderson, Cunningham, Gaskins, Schommer, & the Teachers of the Benchmark School, 1988) which confirmed for me that decoding was neither a letter-by-letter sounding process nor a rule-based, jargon-filled process. My observations of the children I had taught as well as the research I carried out convinced me that, when readers come to unfamiliar words, they do a fast search through their cognitive word stores for similar words with the same letters in the same places. They then use these analogs to come up with a possible pronunciation that they try out and cross-check with meaning.

I understood finally that when I complained that my first graders knew the rules but didn't use them, I was probably right! The rules describe the system. The brain, however, is not a rule applier but a pattern detector. I also understood why teaching children linguistic patterns or "word families" was a powerful strategy if you could get them to use these spelling patterns to write and read words in meaningful texts.

By 1982, ten years after Rod and Erin had learned to read, I had figured out how they did it. Combining word-family instruction with reading and writing in which they were encouraged to use rhyming words to figure out how to pronounce or spell unknown words taught them to look for patterns in words and, most importantly, that there were patterns to be found when they looked. Looking up big words in the dictionary respelling key forced them to look carefully at all the letters in the words (so that they could find them in the dictionary) and the analogs contained in the respelling key convinced them that there were patterns to be found in big words, too!

What We Know about How Good Readers Read Words

We know a great deal more about how word recognition occurs than can be explained in this section. The theory that explains the incredibly fast ability of the brain to recognize words and associate them with meaning is called parallel distributed processing. This theory is complex but its most important tenets are easily understood. Information about a word is gained from its spelling (orthography), its pronunciation (phonology), its meaning (semantics), and the context in which the word occurs. The brain processes these sources of information in parallel, or simultaneously. The brain functions in word recognition, as it does in all other areas, as a pattern detector. Discussion of parallel distributed processing and its implications for word identification can be found in McClelland and Rumelhart, 1986; Rumelhart and McClelland, 1986; and Seidenberg and McClelland, 1989. The theory is translated and explained simply and elegantly in Adams (1990). Beyond the fact that the brain responds to many sources of information in parallel and that it functions as a pattern detector, the following specific facts seem particularly pertinent to the question of what kind of phonics instruction we should have.

Readers Look at Virtually All of the Words and Almost All the Letters in Those Words (McConkie, Kerr, Reddix, & Zola, 1987; Rayner & Pollatsek, 1989).
For many years, it was generally believed that sophisticated readers sampled text. Based on predictions about what words and letters they would see, readers were thought to look at the words and letters just enough to see if their predictions were confirmed. Eye-movement research carried out with computerized tracking has proven that, in reality, readers look at every word and almost every letter of each word. The amount of time spent processing each letter is incredibly small, only a few hundredths of a second. The astonishingly fast letter recognition for letters within familiar words and patterns is explained by the fact that our brains expect certain letters to occur in sequence with other letters.

Readers Usually Recode Printed Words into Sound (McCutchen, Bell, France, & Perfetti, 1991; Tannenhaus, Flanigan, & Seidenberg, 1980).
Although it is possible to read without any internal speech, we rarely do. Most of the time, as we read, we think the words in our mind. This phonological information is then checked with the information we received visually by analyzing the word for familiar spelling patterns. Saying the words aloud or thinking the words also seems to perform an important function in holding the words in auditory memory until enough words are read to create meaning.

Readers Recognize Most Words Immediately and Automatically without Using Context (LaBerge & Samuels, 1974; Nicholson, 1991; Stanovich, 1991). Good readers use context to see if what they are reading makes sense. Context is also important for disambiguating the meaning of some words (I had a *ball* throwing the *ball* at the *ball.*) Occasionally, readers use context to figure out what the word is. Most of the time, however, words are identified based on their familiar spelling and the association of that spelling with a pronunciation. Context comes into play after, not before, the word is identified based on the brain's processing of the letter-by-letter information it receives. Several studies have found that poor readers rely more on context than good readers.

Readers Accurately and Quickly Pronounce Infrequent, Phonetically Regular Words (Hogaboam & Perfetti, 1978). When presented with unfamiliar but phonetically regular words, good readers immediately and seemingly effortlessly assign them a pronunciation. The ability to quickly and accurately pronounce phonetically regular words that are not sight words is a task that consistently discriminates between good and poor readers.

Readers Use Spelling Patterns and Analogy to Decode Words (Adams, 1990; Goswami & Bryant, 1990; Moustafa, 1997). The answer to the question of whether phonics should be taught in a synthetic or analytic manner seems to be neither. Synthetic approaches generally teach children to go letter by letter, assigning a pronunciation to each letter and then blending the individual letters together. Analytic approaches teach rules and are usually filled with confusing jargon. (The *e* on the end makes the vowel long.) Brain research, however, suggests that the brain is a pattern detector, not a rule applier and that, while we look at single letters, we are looking at them and considering all the letter patterns we know. Successfully decoding a word occurs when the brain recognizes a familiar spelling pattern or, if the pattern itself is not familiar, the brain searches through its store of words with similar patterns.

To decode the unfamiliar word *knob,* for example, the child who knew many words that began with *kn* would immediately assign to the *kn* the "n" sound. The initial *kn* would be stored in the brain as a spelling pattern. If the child knew only a few other words with *kn* and hadn't read these words very often, that child would probably not have *kn* as a known spelling pattern and, thus, would have to do a quick search for known words that began with *kn*. If the child found the words *know* and *knew* and then tried this same sound on the unknown word *knob,* that child would have used the analogy strategy. Likewise, the child might know the pronunciation for *ob* because of having correctly read so many words containing the *ob* spelling pattern or might have had to access some words with *ob* to use them to come up with the pronunciation. The child who had no stored spelling patterns for *kn* or *ob* and no known words to access and compare to would be unlikely to successfully pronounce the unknown word *knob.*

Readers Divide Big Words as They See Them Based on Interletter Frequencies (Mewhort & Campbell, 1981; Seidenberg, 1987). The research on syllabication rules show that it is quite possible to know the rules and still be unable to quickly and accurately pronounce novel polysyllabic words and equally possible to be able to pronounce them and not know the rules. Good readers "chunk" or divide words into manageable units. They do this based on the brain's incredible knowledge of which letters usually go together in words. If you did not recognize the word *midnight* in print, you would divide it as you saw it, between the *d* and the *n*. For the word *Madrid*, however, you would divide after the *a*, leaving the *dr* together. Interletter frequency theory explains this neatly by pointing out that the letters *dr* often occur together in syllables in words you know (*drop, dry, Dracula*). Words with the letters *dn* in the same syllable are almost nonexistent. This also explains why beginners might pronounce *f-a-t-h-e-r* as "fat her" but children who have some words from which the brain can generate interletter frequencies will leave the *th* together and pronounce "father."

Although summarizing what the brain does to identify words runs the risk of oversimplification, it seems necessary before considering what we know about instruction. As we read, we look very quickly at almost all letters of each word. For most words, this visual information is recognized as a familiar pattern with which a spoken word is identified and pronounced. Words we have read before are instantly recognized as we see them. Words we have not read before are almost instantly pronounced based on spelling patterns the brain has seen in other words. If the word is a big word, the brain uses its interletter frequency knowledge (based on all the words it knows) to chunk the word into parts whose letter patterns can then be compared. Meaning is accessed through visual word recognition, but the sound of the word supports the visual information and helps to hold the word in memory.

What We Know about How Children Learn to Read Words

At present, we know more about how the word identification process works than we do about how children learn to do it. Here are some research-based findings that should have an impact on instruction.

Children from Literate Homes Have Over 1,000 Hours of Informal Reading and Writing Encounters before Coming to School (Adams, 1990). We have always known that children who were read to came to school more ready, willing, and able to learn to read. In the past decade, however, findings from emergent literacy research have made it clear that the reading/writing encounters many children have include more than just a bedtime story. Estimates are that children from literate homes experience almost an hour each day of informal reading and writing encounters—being read to, trying to read a favorite book, watching someone write a thank-you letter, trying to write, manipulating magnetic letters, talking with someone about environmental print such as grocery/restaurant labels, signs, and so forth. From these encounters, the children learn a tremendous amount of critical information. They know what reading and writing are really for and that you use words and letters. They know that you have to write these words and letters in a particular way, from top to bottom and left to right (though they often don't know this jargon). They also learn some words—important words like their name and the name of their pet dog and favorite fast-food restaurant. They learn the names of many of the letters of the alphabet and write these letters, usually in capital form. In addition to learning that words are made up of letters, which they can see, they somehow figure out that words are also made up of sounds, which they can't see.

Phonemic Awareness Is Important to Success in Beginning Reading

(Bryant, Bradley, Maclean, & Crossland, 1989; Ehri & Nunes, 2002). One of the understandings that many children gain from early reading and writing encounters is the understanding that words are made up of sounds. These sounds are not separate and distinct. In fact, their existence is quite abstract. Phonemic awareness has many levels and includes the ability to hear whether or not words rhyme, to know what word you would have if you removed a sound, and to manipulate phonemes to form different words. Phonemic awareness seems to be developed through lots of exposure to nursery rhymes and books that make words sound fun. Although children may be able to learn some letter sounds before they develop phonemic awareness, phonemic awareness must be present before children can manipulate those sounds as they try to read and write words.

Children Who Can Decode Well Learn Sight Words Better (Ehri, 1991; Jorm

& Share, 1983; Stanovich & West, 1989). Research indicates that the sight word versus phonics debate lacks reality when you consider how children learn words. When a new word is encountered for the first time, it is usually decoded. In decoding the word, the child forms phonological access routes for that word into memory. These access routes are built using knowledge of grapheme–phoneme correspondences that connect letters in spelling to phonemes in pronunciations of the words. The letters are processed as visual symbols for the phonemes and the sequence of letters is retained in memory as an alphabetic, phonological representation of the word. When the child encounters that word again, the connections between letters and phonemes is strengthened. Eventually, the spelling is represented in memory and the word is instantly recognized—but that instant recognition was based on some prior phonological processing. So words that were originally decoded come to be recognized as wholes and words originally taught as wholes must be studied letter by letter in order to be instantly recognized. The phonics versus sight word debate should be laid to rest.

The Division of Words into Onset and Rime Is a Psychological Reality

(Trieman, 1985). In the 1934 edition of *Reading and Literature in the Elementary School*, Paul McKee discussed activities to help children decode words and indicated that there was mixed opinion as to whether it was best to start with the initial letters and then add the end (*sa-t*) or to keep the final letters together and add the beginning (*s-at*). Expressing some uncertainty, he did take a stand and recommend the latter. Teachers were encouraged to do word activities in which they took a known word and then changed the initial letters—*hand, sand, band, grand, stand.* Amazingly, he recommended that phonics instruction include "other tools such as analogy. . . ." For example, when confronted with the strange word *meat*, he may derive its pronunciation by proper associations gathered from the known words *eat* and *met* (p. 189).

McKee's intuitive understanding of the reading process in 1934 led him to recommend what researchers confirmed 50 years later. Syllables are the most distinct sound units in English, and children and adults find it much easier to divide syllables into their onsets (all letters before the vowel) and rimes (the vowel and what follows) than into any other units. Thus, *Sam* is more easily divided into *S-am* than into *Sa-m* or *S-a-m*. It is easier and quicker for people to change *Sam* to *ham* and *jam* than it is to change *Sam* to *sat* and *sad*. The psychological reality of onset and rime confirms the age-old practice of teaching word families and spelling patterns.

Lots of Successful Reading Is Essential for Readers to Develop Automaticity and Rapid Decoding

(Juel, 1990; Samuels, 2002; Stanovich & West, 1989). The major observable variable that separates good readers from poor readers is that good readers read a lot more and, when they are reading, they recognize most of the words instantly and automatically. If you recognize almost all the words, an unfamiliar word gets your immediate attention and you will stop and figure it out. Lots of easy reading in which most words are immediately recognized is essential for both the development of instantly recognized words and the ability and willingness to decode the occasional unfamiliar word. Many factors—including topic familiarity, text and picture support, number of unfamiliar words, and teacher support—interact to determine how easy or difficult a particular book is for a particular child.

Children Need to Apply Phonics to Their Reading but Not Necessarily in Highly Decodable Text

(Cunningham & Cunningham, 2002). The first time you encounter an unfamiliar-in-print word, you don't recognize it immediately. You have to figure out what it is. You might decode it or you might hear someone pronounce it.

The next time you see that word you might remember having seen it but you might not remember what it is. Again, you could figure it out or you could ask someone, "What's that word?" Depending on how many repetitions you need to learn words (and that varies greatly from child to child) and on how important and distinctive the word is (most children learn *pizza* and *dinosaur* with few repetitions!), you will eventually get to the point where you "just know it." A sight word, like a good friend, is recognized instantly anywhere. Recognizing most of the word instantly—and only having to stop and figure out the occasional word—is what allows us to read quickly and fluently.

Children do need to learn to decode words, but there is a danger in having them figure out all—or almost all—the words as they are beginning to learn to read. The danger is that they will get in the habit of "sounding out" every word—and that is not how good readers read. During the last "phonics era," it was not uncommon to hear children who read like this:

I-t w-i-ll b-e a g--oo--d d--ay.

Many of these children had read these common words—*it, will, be, good,* and *day*— many times and should have recognized them as sight words. But they had gotten into the habit of sounding out every word and habits are hard to break.

Some phonics advocates want to restrict materials beginners read to include only words they can decode and the absolutely necessary sight words. They argue that this will give children lots of practice decoding and require them to use their decoding skills as they read. The call for decodable text is to a great extent a response to the irresponsible beginning reading texts of the last era in which the demand for real literature and real authors resulted in reading books that even average readers couldn't read! Teachers and publishers are now realizing that beginning readers need meaningful text that they are able to read. There is research evidence to support providing children with lots of "readable" text"—text they can read easily. Having some decodable words and the strategies to decode those words is part of what makes text readable. But there are no studies that suggest that children learn to read better when the text they are reading is restricted to only those words they have been taught to decode.

Children Need Systematic Phonics Instruction but There Is No Best Systematic Approach (National Reading Panel, 2000; Stahl, Duffy-Hester, & Stahl, 1998). The question of how best to teach phonics is an important one and should not be too difficult to answer. In reality, it is quite difficult. Historically, there are three kinds of approaches to phonics—synthetic, analytic, and analogic.

Synthetic phonics programs teach sounds first and children read words that contain those sounds. When children have learned the short sound for *a* and the sound for *m, t,* and *b,* they read the words *am, at, mat, bat, tab, tam,* and *bam.* As more sounds are added, more "decodable" words are read. The first "stories" the children read contain only words with the sounds they have been taught and a few necessary high-frequency words such as *the, is,* and *on.* "Real" stories are read aloud to the children but the stories they read are intended primarily to practice decoding. Children also write but their writing is limited to the words that contain the sounds they have been taught. Decodable text generally plays a large role in synthetic phonics programs.

Analytic programs begin by teaching children some words and then helping children to "analyze" those words and learn phonics rules and generalizations based on those words. The phonics in most basal readers is analytic and children read stories using sight words, context, and prediction as they are learning the phonics rules. Phonics is taught gradually over a longer period of time and children are encouraged to read all kinds of text and write about all kinds of topics. Their reading and writing are not controlled by or limited to the sounds they have been taught.

Analogic phonics is also based on words children have learned to read but, rather than teach children phonics rules, children are taught to notice patterns in words and to use the words they know to figure out other words. In an analogic approach to phonics, children would be taught that if you know how to read and spell *cat,* you can also read and spell *bat, rat, hat, sat,* and other rhyming words. Analogic phonics, like analytic phonics, is taught gradually and children's reading and writing are not restricted just to the patterns that they have been taught.

In addition to synthetic, analytic, and analogic approaches, Stahl, Duffy-Hester, and Stahl (1998) identify and review research on two "contemporary" approaches to phonics—spelling-based approaches and embedded phonics approaches. Spelling-based approaches included word sorting (Bear, Invernizzi, Templeton, & Johnston, 2004) and Making Words (Cunningham & Cunningham, 1992). They conclude that "both of these approaches seem to be effective as part of overall approaches to teaching reading" (p. 347).

To explain their conclusion that there is no research-proven, most effective approach to phonics instruction, Stahl, Duffy-Hester, and Stahl (1998) theorized:

> The notion that children construct knowledge about words may explain why the differences among programs are small. As long as one provides early and systematic information about the code, it may not matter very much how one does it. . . . If the information is similar, the learning should be as well. . . . If this information is made available to children, then it may not matter exactly how the instruction occurs. (pp. 350–351)

The National Reading Panel (2000) reached a similar conclusion:

> In teaching phonics explicitly and systematically, several different instructional approaches have been used. These include synthetic phonics, analytic

phonics, embedded phonics, analogy phonics, onset-rime phonics, and phonics through spelling. . . . Phonics-through-spelling programs teach children to transform sounds into letters to write words. Phonics in context approaches teach children to use sound–letter correspondences along with context clues to identify unfamiliar words they encounter in text. Analogy phonics programs teach children to use parts of written words they already know to identify new words. The distinctions between systematic phonics approaches are not absolute, however, and some phonics programs combine two or more of these types of instruction. (pp. 2–89)

The National Reading Panel Report (2000) went on to state that

specific systematic phonics programs are all more effective than non-phonics programs and they do not appear to differ significantly from each other in their effectiveness. (pp. 2–132).

Using a Variety of Phonics Approaches Seems to Matter Most for Struggling Readers McCandliss, Beck, Sandak, and Perfetti (2003) investigated the effectiveness of Isabel Beck's instructional strategy, Word Building, with students who had failed to benefit from traditional phonics instruction. (Word Building is very similar to Making Words, Changing a Hen into a Fox, and Reading/Writing Rhymes, three of the phonics instructional activities in *Phonics They Use.*) They found that the children who received this word-building instruction demonstrated significantly greater improvements on standardized measures of decoding, reading comprehension, and phonological awareness.

Davis (2000) found that spelling-based decoding instruction was as effective as reading-based decoding instruction for all her students but more effective for the children with poor phonological awareness.

A recent study by Juel and Minden-Cupp (2000) confirmed the notion that the most effective phonics instruction for struggling readers was not limited to a single approach. They concluded that the most effective teachers they observed of children who entered first grade with few literacy skills combined systematic letter–sound instruction with onset/rime analogy instruction, and taught these units to application in both reading and writing.

Children's Word Knowledge Is at All Different Levels Children reading on all different levels is a constant concern. The National Reading Panel (2000) report did not offer any research-based solution to this problem but it did acknowledge the universality of the problem and the dilemma all teachers face.

As with any instructional program, there is always the question: "Does one size fit all?" Teachers may be expected to use a particular phonics program with their class, yet it quickly becomes apparent that the program suits some students more than others. In the early grades, children are known to vary greatly in the skills they bring to school. There will be some children who already know the letter–sound correspondences, some children who can decode words, and others who have little or no knowledge. Should teachers proceed through the program and ignore these students? (pp. 2–136)

Summary: The Research and Phonics They Use

The activities described in *Phonics They Use* provide multiple and varied opportunities for children to obtain the information they need to successfully decode and spell words. The activities have different focuses and proceed differently precisely because there is no best way to teach phonics. The activities are multilevel so that children who are at different points in their word knowledge and who need different amounts of information can all learn something about how words work from the same activity. The activities all stress transfer because the only phonics knowledge that matters is the knowledge children actually use when they are reading and writing. There is no research-proven best way to teach phonics, but research does indicate that children who engage in a variety of phonics activities and in lots of reading and writing become better readers and writers.

chapter 15

Phonics Jargon— For Teachers Only!

In the midst of the current phonics frenzy, various groups have decided we need to test teachers' phonics knowledge. Unfortunately, the items on these phonics knowledge tests have absolutely nothing to do with how readers actually use phonics. The test items test knowledge of jargon and rules. Test items often ask teachers to recognize words with inflected endings, derivational suffixes, bound and free roots, and open and closed syllables. You may be asked to count syllables, speech sounds, and morphemes. Syllables are easy to count but your answer might be wrong depending on your dialect. Dialect makes a difference for speech sounds, too.

Passing such phonics knowledge tests may be mandated but that doesn't mean that knowing this stuff makes you a better teacher generally or even a better phonics teacher. Although some studies have reported that many teachers fail such tests of phonics knowledge, there are no studies that demonstrate that teachers who pass such tests actually can and do teach more effectively or even teach phonics more effectively. If you have to take the test, this chapter will help you learn the jargon needed to pass it. In return for my time and page space to include this "study aid" for you, I ask two things. First, please don't inflict all this jargon on the children you teach. The tests they take usually determine if they can decode words, not if they know the jargon. Second, write to whoever decided you should have to take the test and ask for the "scientific" evidence that acquiring such knowledge improves teaching or learning.

affixes   A term that includes both prefixes and suffixes. *Un* and *ible* are both affixes.

base word   (sometimes called *root* or *root word*) A word to which prefixes and/or suffixes can be added.

breve   A diacritic mark (´) put over a vowel to indicate it has the "short" sound.

compound words   Combinations of two words.

consonant   A letter that is not a vowel. *Y* can be a consonant (*yes*) or vowel (*my, Danny*).

consonant blends   Two or more consonants in which you can hear both sounds blended. The word *blend* begins and ends with a consonant blend. *Squall* and *scrub* begin with blends. *Burst* ends with one. The words *comb* and *down* have two consonants at the end but they are not blends because you only hear one of them.

consonant clusters   Another term for *consonant blends*.

consonant digraph   Two consonant letters with a single sound different from that of either of the letters, *sh, ch, wh, th, ph.* (*Digraph* ends with the digraph *ph.*) The tricky part here is that silent letters don't count. *Write, knock,* and *gnu* do not begin with digraphs. I don't know what you call *wr, kn,* and *gn,* but I am sure it doesn't matter if you can produce the right sound when you see them (rarely) in a word.

consonant *le* syllables   Syllables that end in consonant *le* as in *table.*

decode   To "figure out the pronunciation" of a word.

derivational suffix   A suffix that changes the word meaning. The new word has a separate dictionary entry. The most common of these derivational suffixes include *less, ful,* and *er* (person or thing).

diphthong   Two vowel letters that produce a "gliding" sound, *oi, oy, ou, ow* (except the *ou* in *soul* and *ow* in *tow* are not diphthongs because each has a single sound).

encode   To write or spell a word.

homographs   Words with the same spelling but different pronunciations and meanings as in "She did not shed a *tear* when she saw the *tear* in her new dress."

homophones   (also called homonyms) Words with different spellings and meanings that are pronounced the same as in "It was *too* late *to* get *to* the *two*-o'clock show on time."

inflected endings   (sometimes called *inflectional suffixes*) Endings added to words to change where in sentences they are used. The most common inflected endings are *s*, *ing*, *ed*, *ly*, and *er/est* (comparative). It may help you to remember that the phrase *inflected endings* has three of them—the *ed* in *inflected*, and the *ing* and *s* on *endings*.

long vowels   Vowels that "say their names." They can be spelled in lots of ways. If you are asked to think of all the ways you could spell a vowel such as "long *a*," think of words you know such as *rain, base, they, tray, eight, break,* and *vacation.* Remember that other vowels can spell the sound you are aiming for as in *they* and *weigh* and think of polysyllabic words as in *vacation.*

macron   A diacritic mark (—) put over a vowel to indicate it has the "long" sound.

morphemes   Meaning-bearing units in a word, usually roots, prefixes, and suffixes. Many words have multiple morphemes. *Believe* has one morpheme (the *be* in *believe* is not a morpheme): *believer* = 2; *believers* = 3; *unbelievers* = 4.

onsets   All the beginning letters up to the vowel: *sp*end; *kn*ow; *str*ing; *b*and.

phonemes   (also called *speech sounds*) The smallest units of speech. *Bad* has three phonemes. *Good* has three phonemes—but four letters. To count phonemes, say the words and pretend you are Dan Rather, Tom Brokaw, or Peter Jennings. In my New England dialect, *park* has only three speech sounds (New Englanders don't do *r*'s!), whereas Jim (husband) insists it has four. Use the "pretend you're a TV anchor" strategy and Jim is right. To determine phonemes, ignore letters and talk anchorese and count (and pray!). Here are a few examples: *ax* = 3; *sing* = 3; *think* = 4; *brought* = 4; *shine* = 3; *through* = 3; *spacious* = 6.

phonemic awareness   The ability to manipulate the sounds in words.

phonograms   Rimes in printed words.

phonology   The study of speech sounds.

prefix   Something before a root word that usually changes meaning. The prefix in *unhappy* is *un*. In *uniform*, the prefix is *uni*. In *endure*, the prefix is *en*—but *en* is not a prefix in *end* or *enemy*.

r-**controlled vowels**   Vowels in which the vowel sound is affected by the *r* as in *car, her, girl, working,* and *urgent.*

rimes   (also called phonograms and word families) The vowel and following consonants within a syllable.

roots   Sometimes called *base words*. Roots are often of Latin or Greek origin. Roots are *bound* if they are not words by themselves. They are *free* when they are words by themselves. The word *telegraph* has a bound root—*tele* and a free root—*graph*.

schwa   The vowel in an unaccented syllable, sounds kind of like "uh." The schwa sound is underlined in these words: *alone, harmony, extra, celebrate, vacation.*

sight word   Another term for a high-frequency word.

silent *e* syllables   Syllables that end in silent *e* as in *decide*.

soft *c* and *g*   *C* and *g* are sometimes pronounced like *s* and *j* when followed by *e, i,* or *y* as in *cent, city, cyclone, gentle, gist,* and *gym*. These are sometimes called "soft" sounds.

speech sounds   Phonemes.

stem   Root or base word.

structural analysis   Identifying word parts such as compound words, affixes, roots, and syllables.

suffix   Something added to the end of a base or root word. Some suffixes are inflectional and some are derivational.

syllables   Units of sound that contain a vowel and may be preceded or followed by one or more consonants. *Pat* has one syllable; *Alice* has two. *Cunningham* has three. Open syllables end in a vowel and often have a long vowel sound—the *ti* in *tiger*. Closed syllables end in a consonant and often have a short vowel sound—the *Tig* in *Tigger*. If you have to explain why there is a double *m* in *comma*, explain that the first *m* closes the syllable, thus assuring its short vowel sound. With only one *m*, it would have the long sound as in *coma*.

vowels   Letters that are not consonants: *a, e, i, o, u,* and sometimes *y*.

vowel digraphs   Two vowel letters that make one sound. *Coat, yield, tie,* and *soul* have vowel digraphs.

vowel team syllables   Syllables that have two vowels with one sound (vowel digraphs).

words of Greek origin   These words can be easily recognized by their *y* as in *Olympics,* their *ch* as in *choir,* their *ph* as in *phonics,* and Greek roots such as *psyche* and *ology*.

References

Adams, M. J. (1990). *Beginning to read: Thinking and learning about print.* Cambridge, MA: MIT Press.

Bear, D. B., Invernizzi, M., Templeton, S., & Johnston, F. (2004). *Words their way* (3rd ed.). New York: Macmillan/Merrill.

Bryant, P. E., Bradley, L., Maclean, M., & Crossland, I. (1989). Nursery rhymes, phonological skills and reading. *Journal of Child Language, 16,* 407–428.

Caldwell, J. (2002). *Reading assessment: A primer for teachers and tutors.* New York: Guilford.

Clarke, L. K. (1988). Invented versus traditional spelling in first graders' writings: Effects on learning to spell and read. *Research in the Teaching of English, 22,* 281–309.

Clay, M. M. (1985). *The early detection of reading difficulties* (3rd ed.). Portsmouth, NH: Heinemann.

Cunningham, P. M. (1975–76). Investigating a synthesized theory of mediated word identification. *Reading Research Quarterly, 11,* 127–143.

Cunningham, P. M. (1979). A compare/contrast theory of mediated word identification. *The Reading Teacher, 32,* April, 774–778.

Cunningham, P. M. (1980). Applying a compare/contrast process to identifying polysyllabic words. *Journal of Reading Behavior, 12,* 213–223.

Cunningham, P. M. (1990). The Names Test: A quick assessment of decoding ability. *The Reading Teacher, 44,* 124–129.

Cunningham, P. M. (2000). *Systematic sequential phonics they use.* Greensboro, NC: Carson-Dellosa.

Cunningham, P. M. (2003). *Big words for big kids.* Greensboro, NC: Carson-Dellosa.

Cunningham, P. M., & Allington, R. L. (2003). *Classrooms that work: They can all read and write* (3rd ed.). New York: Longman.

Cunningham, P. M., & Cunningham, J. W. (1992). Making words: Enhancing the invented spelling–decoding connection. *The Reading Teacher, 46,* 106–107.

Cunningham, P. M., & Cunningham, J. W. (2002). What we know about how to teach phonics. In A. E. Farstrup & S. J. Samuels (Eds.), *What research has to say about reading instruction* (3rd ed., pp. 87–109). Newark, DE: International Reading Association.

Cunningham, P. M., & Guthrie, F. M. (1982). Teaching decoding skills to educable mentally handicapped children. *The Reading Teacher, 35,* February, 554–559.

Cunningham, P. M., & Hall, D. P. (1998). *Month-by-month phonics for upper grades: A second chance for struggling readers and students learning English.* Greensboro, NC: Carson-Dellosa.

Cunningham, P. M., & Hall, D. P. (2003). *Reading/writing complex rhymes.* Greensboro, NC: Carson-Dellosa.

Cunningham, P. M., & Hall, D. P. (2003). *Reading/writing simple rhymes.* Greensboro, NC: Carson-Dellosa.

Dale, E., & O'Rourke, J. (1981) *The living word vocabulary.* Chicago: Worldbook.

Davis, L. H. (2000). The effects of rime-based analogy training on word reading and spelling of first-grade children with good and poor phonological awareness (Doctoral dissertation, Northwestern University, 2000). *Dissertation Abstracts International, 61,* 2253A.

Duffelmeyer, F. A., Kruse, A. E., Merkley, D. J., & Fyfe, S. A. (1994). Further validation and enhancement of the Names Test. *The Reading Teacher, 48,* 118–128.

Ehri, L. C. (1991). Development of the ability to read words. In R. Barr, M. L. Kamil, P. B. Mosenthal, & P. D. Pearson, *Handbook of reading research* (Vol. 2, pp. 383–417). White Plains, NY: Longman.

Ehri, L. C., & Nunes, S. R. (2002). The role of phonemic awareness in learning to read. In A. E. Farstrup & S. J. Samuels (Eds.), *What research has to say about reading instruction* (3rd ed., pp. 110–139). Newark, DE: International Reading Association.

Elkonin, D. B. (1973). Reading in the USSR. In J. Downing (Ed.), *Comparative reading* (pp. 551–579). New York: Macmillan.

Fielding, L., & Roller, C. (1992). Making difficult books accessible and easy books acceptable. *The Reading Teacher, 45,* 678–685.

Fry, E., Fountoukidis, D. L., & Polk, J. K. (1985). *The new reading teacher's book of lists.* Englewood Cliffs, NJ: Prentice-Hall.

Gaskins I. W., Downer, M. A., Anderson, R. C., Cunningham, P. M., Gaskins, R. W., Schommer, M., & Teachers of the Benchmark School. (1988). A metacognitive approach to phonics: Using what you know to decode what you don't know. *Remedial and Special Education, 9,* 36–41.

Goswami, U., & Bryant, P. (1990). *Phonological skills and learning to read.* East Sussex, UK: Erlbaum Associates.

Harris, A. J., & Sipay, E. R. (1990). *How to increase reading ability* (8th ed.). New York: Longman.

Henderson, E. H. (1990). *Teaching spelling* (2nd ed.). Boston: Houghton Mifflin.

Hogaboam, T., & Perfetti, C. A. (1978). Reading skill and the role of verbal experience in decoding. *Journal of Verbal Learning and Verbal Behavior, 70,* 717–729.

Jorm, A. F., & Share, D. L. (1983). Phonological recoding and reading acquisition. *Applied Psycholinguistics, 4,* 103–147.

Juel, C. (1990). Effects of reading group assignment on reading development in first and second grade. *Journal of Reading Behavior, 22,* 233–254.

Juel, C., & Minden-Cupp, C. (2000). Learning to read words: Linguistic units and instructional strategies. *Reading Research Quarterly, 35,* 458–492.

LaBerge, D., & Samuels, S. J. (1974). Toward a theory of automatic information processing in reading. *Cognitive Psychology, 6,* 293–323.

McCandliss, B., Beck, I. L., Sandak, R., & Perfetti, C. (2003). Focusing attention on decoding for children with poor reading skills: Design and preliminary tests of the Word Building intervention. *Scientific Studies of Reading, 7*, 75–104.

McClelland, J. L., & Rumelhart, D. E. (Eds.) (1986). *Parallel distributed processing, Vol. 2: Psychological and biological models.* Cambridge, MA: MIT Press.

McConkie, G. W., Kerr, P. W., Reddix, M. D., & Zola, D. (1987). *Eye movement control during reading: The location of initial eye fixations on words.* Technical Report No. 406. Champaign, IL: Center for the Study of Reading, University of Illinois.

McCutchen, D., Bell, L. C., France, I. M. & Perfetti, C. A. (1991). Phoneme-specific interference in reading: The tongue-twister effect revisited. *Reading Research Quarterly, 26*, 87–103.

McKee, P. (1934). *Reading and literature in the elementary school.* Boston: Houghton Mifflin.

Mewhort, D. J. K., & Campbell, A. J. (1981). Toward a model of skilled reading: An analysis of performance in tachistoscoptic tasks. In G. E. MacKinnon & T. G. Walker (Eds.), *Reading Research: Advances in Theory and Practice* (Vol. 3, 39–118). New York: Academic Press.

Moustafa, M. (1997) *Beyond traditional phonics.* Portsmouth: NH: Heinemann.

National Reading Panel (2000). *Teaching children to read: An evidence-based assessment of the scientific research literature on reading and its implications for reading instruction: Reports of the subgroups* (National Institute of Health Pub. No. 00-4754). Washington, DC: National Institute of Child Health and Human Development.

Nicholson, T. (1991). Do children read words better in context or in lists? A classic study revisited. *Journal of Educational Psychology, 83*, 444–450.

Pearson, P. D. (1993). Teaching and learning reading: A research perspective. *Language Arts, 70*, 502–511.

Perfetti, C. A. (1991). The psychology, pedagogy, and politics of reading. *Psychological Science, 2*, 70, 71–76.

Pinnell, G. S., & Fountas, I. (1998). *Word matters.* Portsmouth: NH: Heinemann.

Rasinski, T. V. (2003). *The fluent reader.* New York: Scholastic.

Rasinski, T. V., & Padak, N. D. (1998). How elementary students referred for compensatory reading instruction perform on school-based measures of word recognition, fluency and comprehension. *Reading Psychology, 19*, 185–216.

Rasinski, T. V., & Padak, N. D. (2001). *From phonics to fluency.* New York: Longman.

Rayner, K., & Pollatsek, A. (1989). *The psychology of reading.* Englewood Cliffs, NJ: Prentice Hall.

Rumelhart, D. E., & McClelland, J. L. (Eds.) (1986). *Parallel distributed processing, Vol. 1: Psychological and biological models.* Cambridge, MA: MIT Press.

Samuels, S. J. (2002). Reading fluency: Its development and assessment. In A. E. Farstrup & S. J. Samuels (Eds.), *What research has to say about reading instruction* (3rd ed., pp. 166–183). Newark, DE: International Reading Association.

Seidenberg, M. S. (1987). Sublexical structures in visual word recognition: Access units or orthographic redundancy. In M. Coltheart (Ed.), *Attention and performance XII: The psychology of reading* (pp. 245–263). Hillsdale, NJ: Erlbaum Associates.

Seidenberg, M. S., & McClelland, J. L. (1989). A distributed, developmental model of word recognition and naming. *Psychological Review, 96*, 523–568.

Stahl, S. A., Duffy-Hester, A. M., & Stahl, K. A. (1998). Everything you wanted to know about phonics (but were afraid to ask). *Reading Research Quarterly, 33*, 338–355.

Stanovich, K. E. (1991). Word recognition: Changing perspectives. In R. Barr, M. L. Kamil, P. B. Mosenthal, & P. D. Pearson, (Eds.), *Handbook of reading research* (Vol. 2, pp. 418–452). White Plains, NY: Longman.

Stanovich, K. E., & West, R. F. (1989). Exposure to print and orthographic processing. *Reading Research Quarterly, 24*, 402–433.

Sulzby, E., Teale, W. H., & Kamberelis, G. (1989). Emergent writing in the classroom: Home and school connections. In D. S. Strickland & L. M. Morrow (Eds.), *Emerging literacy: Young children learn to read and write.* Newark, DE: International Reading Association.

Tannenhaus, M. K., Flanigan, H., & Seidenberg, M. S. (1980). Orthographic and phonological code activation in auditory and visual word recognition. *Memory and Cognition, 8,* 513–520.

Teale, W. H., & Sulzby, E. (1991). Emergent literacy. In R. Barr, M. Kamil, P. Mosenthal, & P. D. Pearson (Eds.), *Handbook of reading research* (Vol. 2, pp. 418–452). New York: Longman.

Trieman, R. (1985). Onsets and rimes as units of spoken syllables: Evidence from children. *Journal of Experimental Child Psychology, 39,* 161–181.

White, T., Sowell, J., & Yanagihara, A. (1989). Teaching elementary students to use word-part clues. *The Reading Teacher, 42,* 302–308.

Wylie, R. E., & Durrell, D. D. (1970). Teaching vowels through phonograms. *Elementary English, 47,* 787–791.

Yopp, H. K. (1995). A test for assessing phonemic awareness for young children. *The Reading Teacher, 49,* 20–29.

 # Children Books Cited

(In addition to books in boxes on pages pp. 31, 35, 43, 45, and 104.)

Are You My Mother? by P. D. Eastman (Random House, 1960)

Brown Bear, Brown Bear, What Do You See? by Bill Martin Jr. (Holt, 1983)

Good Night Moon by Margaret Wise Brown (Scholastic, 1989)

Hattie and the Fox by Mem Fox (Simon and Schuster, 1988)

I Wish That I Had Duck Feet by Dr. Seuss (Random House, 1972)

Kinderrhymes—24 titles, including *Rhymes with Cat, Rhymes with Cap,* and *Rhymes with King* (Rigby, 1998).

My Nose Is a Hose by Kent Salisbury (McClanahan, 1997)

There's a Bug in My Mug by Kent Salisbury (McClanahan, 1997)

Things I Like by Anthony Browne (Houghton Mifflin, 1996)

Tog the Dog (1986), *Jen the Hen* (1985), *Mig the Pig* (1984), and *Pat the Cat* (1993) by Colin and Jacqui Hawkins (Putnam)

Zoo Looking by Mem Fox (Mondo, 1996)

Index